T0381445

Bound to God in Christ Jesus

From Slavery to Sin to Slavery to Christ in Romans 6

NATHAN RANDAL TRITCH

WestBow
PRESS®
A DIVISION OF THOMAS NELSON
& ZONDERVAN

WestBow Press books may be ordered through
booksellers or by contacting:

WestBow Press
A Division of Thomas Nelson & Zondervan
1663 Liberty Drive
Bloomington, IN 47403
www.westbowpress.com
844-714-3454

ISBN: 979-8-3850-4016-2 (sc)
ISBN: 979-8-3850-4015-5 (e)

Print information available on the last page.

WestBow Press rev. date: 01/20/2025

This proposal is a reworked manuscript for an intended audience; revised, edited, and reformatted MA Theology thesis *Bound to God in Christ Jesus: From Slavery to Sin to Slavery to God in Christ in Romans 6* submitted to the Faculty of Christ College, Concordia Irvine, CA, June 2022; Slightly edited version Independently published with Xulon Press Elite, 2024.

CONTENTS

Man of Sorrows with Hands Bound (1512),
Drypoint by Albrecht Dürer

Introduction

Contemporary American citizens depict slavery as evil because of forced oppression and the captivity of people groups through the ages. Slavery in the context of current American culture always seems bad and even evil. Yet, for Christians of all generations, slavery is Paul's language for the Baptized into Christ laid out in Romans 6. Through careful examination of slavery in Romans 6, the contemporary reader should be able to adopt a more productive understanding of biblical and spiritual slavery. Slavery language is important because our understanding of slavery is explicably shaped by the United States' fraught and unsettling history. Therefore, how can a loving God ask us to be slaves? This thesis helps answer those concerns by putting slavery in its correct context and discussing the implications of being a slave of righteousness.

U.S. history reveals the Civil War was fought, in part, over slavery and included the freeing of all slaves in the Union.[1] Injustice took the form of slavery through involuntary and obligatory capture, trading, and forced labor of African people living under extreme, poor, and harsh conditions

---

[1] For a deeper theological overview and history of the Civil War, see Mark Noll, *The Civil War as a Theological Crisis*, (North Carolina: The University of North Carolina Press, 2006).

without moral care, rights, freedom, and protection as citizens.[2] This slavery was not an isolated incident, but rather a policy incorporated within the U.S. It is estimated that approximately fifteen million people were transported to the Americas from Africa as slaves during the slave trade.[3] This image of slavery has dominated conversations about even the use of the word "slavery," making its use, even in positive contexts, unpalatable. However, the image of slavery can shape one's understanding of the slavery depicted in the Scriptures, which then shapes the present.[4]

---

[2] Considering the language of "justice" and "injustice" today, its abuses by the world of social criticism, Marxist ideologies, i.e. social justice, CRT, DEI, a highly recommended critique of these ideologies, see Jon Harris, *Christianity and Social Justice: Religions in Conflict* (Ann Arbor, Michigan: Reformation Zion Publishing, 2021); See Harris' *Christianity and Social Justice* Ch. 6 section, "Social Justice Ethics," under subheading, "The Sources of Evil and Contentment," 120-124, specifically on a brief look at slavery of the Greco Roman era and other helpful insights. For more resources on woke ideology, cf. Voddie T. Baucham, *It's Not Like Being Black* (New York, Regnery Faith, 2024); Baucham, *Fault Lines* (Salem Books, Washington, D.C., 2021); Rev. Paul Dare, *Christians In A Woke World: A Call to Courage, Confession, and Love* (Independently Published, 2021).

[3] Cf. Ralph A. Austen, "The Trans-Saharan Slave Trade: A Tentative Census." *Uncommon Market; Essays in the Economic History of the Atlantic Slave Trade*, ed. by H.A. Gemery and J.A. Hogendorn, 23-76 (1979); "Between 1500 AD and 1890 AD, over twenty-two million (22,000,000) Africans were sold into slavery (R.A. Austen 1979). Seven million (6,856,000) were sold east: with 3,956,000 were sold across the Sahara and 2,900,000 across the Red Sea and the Indian Ocean (R.A. Austen 1979). Fifteen million (15,000,000) were trafficked across the Atlantic. 70% of all Africans sold into slavery in the Americas were transported by Portugal and Britain. For a contrast, 22 million is equivalent to 2x the current population of Sweden." "The Slave Trade in Black Africans," Think Africa, accessed 05/11/2022, https://thinkafrica.net/atlantic-slave-trade/.

[4] The image of slavery in the current culture of American postmillennial ideologies misrepresents historical antiquity, which shapes the present, future, biblical and eschatological realities.

A contemporary reader of the Scriptures would benefit from understanding the context of biblical slavery. The modern perception and misconceptions of "slavery" language are unreflective of biblical reality.[5] Today, slavery remains a real problem and an oversight. John Nordling writes, "Modern slavery, often hidden from the mainstream of societies that otherwise value egalitarian democracy, takes many diverse forms."[6] Current human trafficking (contemporary slavery) is primarily hidden from mainstream society, yet it is no secret and grossly overlooked among Americans and Christians today. Human lives from all over the world are currently trafficked and worked as forced slaves.

This is starkly different from the Bible's discussion of slavery. Slavery in the Greco-Roman period was more

---

[5] The theological reality of spiritual slavery and ancient slavery is the main thought here for reality, "not reflective of reality," instead of the American and worldly experience. Perhaps the philosophical, metaphysical, and ontological concepts of reality and thought throughout history are also of some value and focus on reality. Yet, here is the foremost theological thought in contrast to the past slave trade in America in history and philosophical niceties of the world. Still, the theological reality is the thought and reality above all these realities and primary to the point. History shapes the way one may perceive reality, perhaps, according to their surroundings, environment, emotions, experience, knowledge, past, present, and future as perceptions of reality. Yet, here, the reality discussed in the vastness of realities is intended to be from a spiritual and theological reality of existence and purpose, driving toward a theological perspective of the reality of slavery. So then, slavery in U.S. history, although real as a fact and a reality in that the slave trade happened in time, is the "modern perception" of the reality of U.S. history that misrepresents and overlooks the ultimate theological reality of spiritual slavery. Slavery in ancient history also exceeds beyond the American experience; See Chapter 1 for Earthly Slavery; Chapters 2-4 expand on spiritual slavery.

[6] John G. Nordling, *Philemon,* Concordia Commentary (St. Louis, MO: Concordia Publishing House, 2004), 39.

publicly common and strangely customary for people groups and ethnicities. Rather than today's misapplication of slavery of the sixteenth through nineteenth centuries slave trade, one can see that slavery terminology is used in the Old and New Testaments to speak of varied concepts like salvation, freedom, sinfulness, death, spiritual death, suffering, righteousness, and obedience. Slavery has a multifaceted context; thus, whether worldly or theologically, slavery has existed in every age as both evil and vocational.

Slavery to sin exists as a consequence of sin entering the world. Spiritual slavery to sin and death was introduced in humanity's rebellion toward God. Man's failure to properly respond to God began with rebelling against Yahweh in the garden and resulted in all people being cursed and enslaved to sin and death by Adam and Eve's sin. Since then, mankind has failed in acts and thoughts of rebellion against Yahweh God throughout the ages. However, Yahweh's good and perfect will and Word of Law expose and condemn sin, evil, and oppressive slavery. Sin itself is the true rebellion against Yahweh's holiness and righteousness.

It is helpful to distinguish spiritual slavery from worldly slavery. Worldly slavery involves temporal slavery by mankind and of mankind. Spiritual slavery and physical slavery are true biblical realities. Spiritual slavery and the language of slavery are often used as a metaphor to show the bound and enslaved condition of all mankind to sin as sinful, mortal, and condemned before God Almighty.

Furthermore, both spiritual slavery to sin and, antithetically, a positive slavery to righteousness also have important biblical distinctions. It is, therefore, helpful to distinguish between righteous slavery and slavery to sin. Slavery to sin can only be mankind bound to sin and death. On the other hand, righteous slavery can only be realized when one is bound to God in faith and Baptism into Christ. It expresses how we can be redeemed, freed from sin, and enslaved to Christ and righteousness before God Almighty. These are all true, inescapable realities that extend beyond metaphor and applicable allegorical teachings.

The metaphor of spiritual slavery may sound inappropriate to the American Christian. Yet spiritual slavery displays and captures the bound condition of all mankind before God Almighty, whether of sin and death or of Christ and righteousness. Therefore, what Paul describes as a slave to sin or a slave to righteousness is the Truth as God's Word is Truth (cf. Psalm 119:160; John 17:17), and, ultimately, for the sake of Christ, the Word of God who became flesh (cf. John 1:1, 14; Rev. 19:13). The spiritual slavery to God and righteousness Paul describes in Romans is a biblical Truth. The slave to God in Christ through faith and Baptism conveys a spiritual Truth by God's promise of freedom and His declaration of righteousness and freedom from slavery to sin (cf. Rom 6:7, 18, 22). Spiritual slavery, then, is truly evil for the slave to sin, but good for the slave to Christ.

Although spiritual slavery sounds bad, as if one was not actually free, Christians are thankful slaves of righteousness and God, freed from slavery to sin and bound to Christ Jesus. Jesus Christ took the form of a "δοῦλος[7]–slave"[8] (Phil

---

[7] δοῦλος; "*1401*. dŏulŏs, *doo'-los*; from *1210*; a *slave* (lit. or fig., involving. or vol.; frequently therefore in a qualified sense of *subjection* or *subserviency*):—bond (-man), servant." James Strong, *A Concise Dictionary of the Words in the Greek Testament and The Hebrew Bible* (Bellingham, WA: Logos Bible Software, 2009), 24. Hereafter, JStrong.

[8] Slave – δοῦλος, "[dŏulŏs, *doo'-los*] ... to being under someone's total control, *slavish, servile, subject* ... Ro 6:19" William Arndt, Frederick W. Danker, Walter Bauer, et al., *A Greek-English Lexicon of the New Testament and Other Early Christian Literature*, 3rd ed.

2:7) in the flesh to die for sinful humanity—slaves to sin. Christ died so that "ἄνθρωπος–mankind"[9] could be freed and declared righteous from slavery to sin (Rom 6:7) and death to life and righteousness. Paul makes this clear in Romans 6 how Baptism is unity with Christ, "Knowing this, that our old self [ἄνθρωπος] was crucified with [Christ] in order that the body of sin might be rendered ineffective, [that is,] that we might no longer be enslaved to sin" (6:6; cf. vv. 3-5, 7).[10] Slavery to Christ is a good slavery.

This book uses "slave" for "δοῦλος" rather than "servant" to avoid confusion and to expose the improper use of "servant"

(Chicago: University of Chicago Press, 2000), 259. Hereafter, BDAG; "δοῦλος ... *doulos*; of unc. der.; *a slave*: — bond-servant." Zondervan Bible Publishers, edited by Robert L. Thomas, *The Strongest NASB Exhaustive Concordance* (Grand Rapids, Michigan: Zondervan, 2004), G1401. Hereafter, NASEC. This book largely uses NASEC for Hebrew and Greek Strong's references compared to BDAG. For further δοῦλος – *doulos* definitions and New Testament usage, see, Gerhard Kittel, Gerhard Friedrich and Geoffrey W. Bromiley. *Theological Dictionary of the New Testament: Abridged in One Volume* (Grand Rapids, MI: W.B. Eerdmans, 1985), 182-86; cf. Gerhard Kittel and Geoffrey W. Bromiley. *Theological Dictionary of the New Testament,* vol 2 (Grand Rapids, MI: W.B. Eerdmans, 1964), 261-80; Henry Liddell and Robert Scott, *A Greek-English Lexicon.* 9th ed. (Oxford: Oxford University Press, 1996), 447. See notes 7 and 11.

9   ἄνθρωπος; "*444.* anthrōpŏs, *anth'-ro-pos*; from *435* and ὤψ ōps (the *countenance*; from *3700*); *man-faced*, i.e. a *human* being:—certain, man." JStrong, 12; "ἄνθρωπος ... ① a person of either sex, w. focus on participation in the human race, *a human being* ... ② a member of the human race, w. focus on limitations and weaknesses, *a human being*." BDAG, 81; Cf., ἄνθρωπος, "anthrōpos; prob. from G435 and ὤψ ōps (eye, face); *a man, human, mankind:* — any" NASEC, G444. This book uses humankind, humanity, and mostly "mankind" as the human race for ἄνθρωπος – anthrōpos.

10   Michael P. Middendorf, *Romans 1–8*, ed. Dean O. Wenthe and Curtis P. Giese, *Concordia Commentary* (Saint Louis, MO: Concordia Publishing House, 2013), 443; See note 15 for expl. on English translations used in this book.

for δοῦλος in American translations.[11] The word "servant" is better rendered from "διάκονος."[12] διάκονος often translates, *"assistant, intermediary, agent, courier, servant, minister, deacon,"*[13] and is not in Romans 6. Although "servant" and "slave" are used interchangeably among scholars and translators for δοῦλος in Romans 6, and in specific translations, e.g., King James Version (KJV) and English Standard Version (ESV)[14], the purpose is to keep the definitions of δοῦλος and διάκονος separate and distinct in context. Therefore, maintaining δοῦλος as "slave" throughout this book will challenge the contemporary reader to reconsider slavery in light of various contexts. Ultimately, it expresses the spiritual and eternal reality of slavery to sin and death, but also slavery to righteousness, life, and redemption in Jesus Christ.

Chapter One looks at the context of slavery in the Greco-Roman period of Jesus and Paul. The background of slavery in the Old Testament shows the slavery and redemption of

---

[11] "δοῦλος, ου, ὁ ... ① male slave as an entity in a socioeconomic context, *slave* ('servant' for 'slave' is largely confined to Biblical transl. and early American times [s. OED s.v. servant, 3a and b]; in normal usage at the present time the two words are carefully distinguished [Goodsp., Probs., 77–79]). Opp. ἐλεύθερος 1 Cor 7:21. Lit., in contrast ... ② one who is solely committed to another, slave, subject" BDAG, 260; Cf. notes 7 and 8.

[12] "διάκονος, ου, ὁ, ἡ ... "one who is busy with someth. in a manner that is of assistance to someone ... ① one who serves as an intermediary in a transaction, *agent, intermediary, courier* ... ② one who gets someth. done, at the behest of a superior, assistant." BDAG, 230; Cf., "διάκονος–diakonos; of unc. or.; *a servant, minister:* — deacons." NASEC, G1249. For further *diakonos* definitions and New Testament usage, see, Kittel, Friedrich and Bromiley. *Theological Dictionary of the New Testament: Abridged in One Volume*, 152-55; cf. Kittel and Bromiley, *Theological Dictionary of the New Testament*, vol 2, 81-93; Liddell and Scott, *A Greek-English Lexicon*, 398.

[13] Ibid; Cf. note 12.

[14] E.g., Matt 18:32, both KJV ad ESV translations us "servant" for δοῦλε, which is vocative, sing., masc., for of δοῦλος. The Holy Bible: English Standard Version (Wheaton, IL: Crossway Bibles, 2016).

Israel from slavery, as well as slavery with Israel. Paul then draws on slavery language in Romans 6 to describe the spiritual slavery of mankind before Yahweh. Scripture also introduces the concept of spiritual slavery to righteousness as a Christian vocation bound to God in Christ.

Chapter Two examines spiritual slavery to sin and explains how spiritual slavery is wicked and bad. Jesus confirms, "Truly, truly, I say to you, everyone who commits sin is the slave of sin." (John 8:34 [Legacy Standard Bible]).[15] Slavery to sin is the eternal condition of all mankind.

Chapter Three explores freedom from slavery to sin and God's declaration of righteousness (cf. Rom 6:7, 18, 22). For Jesus says, "So if the Son makes you free, you will be free indeed" (John 8:36). Baptism into Christ's death and resurrection is the means of grace completed for sinners who are now bound to Christ (Rom 6:3-4). Sinners declared righteous and free from slavery to sin are also bound to righteousness and God for the sake of Christ.

Chapter Four culminates this thesis by identifying slavery to God for those redeemed in Christ and what slavery to righteousness looks like. When one is eternally bound to Christ, life's renewal is given to the slave of righteousness. So, how can freedom and slavery exist together in Christ? Jesus took the form of a slave to die for all so they could be declared righteous from slavery to sin and death. In Jesus Christ, one is now a slave of righteousness and bound eternally to God.

---

[15] Unless otherwise noted, this book uses the Legacy Standard Bible (LSB); Legacy Standard Bible (La Habra, CA: The Lockman Foundation/Three Sixteen Publishing, 2021); for all quoted Scripture except Romans 6. Scripture quoted from Romans 6 are translated by Middendorf, *Romans 1–8*, Concordia Commentary (Saint Louis, MO: Concordia Publishing House, 2013), 443, 486. Please note!: LSB in this book is not to be confused with *Lutheran Service Book*; see note 104.

The Crucifixion with the Virgin and Saint John (1624–25),
Oil Painting by Hendrick ter Brugghen

ONE

EARTHLY SLAVERY

This chapter investigates the context of physical slavery, primarily in Paul's day. From a contemporary view, the American experience with slavery ought not to be simplistically equated with the context of slavery in the New Testament era.[16] Slavery in Paul's day was often quite different from the picture one might imagine today. To be sure, ancient slavery and slavery in America were, at times, both cruel and dehumanizing. However, degrading cruelty was not always the case in ancient slavery. Nordling comments, "It is difficult for moderns to think of slavery in objective terms or to consider the idea that—in certain critical respects—ancient slavery could have been quite different from antebellum slavery in America."[17] Voluntary slavery was not uncommon in the ancient world, including

---

[16] "Unlike slavery in the American experience, race had little or nothing to do with slavery in the first century A.D." Nordling, *Philemon*, Concordia Commentary, 69.

[17] Ibid., 42.

1

among God's people, Israel (see Exodus 21; Deuteronomy 15).[18] This is not the image of slavery modern and postmodern readers may expect today.

Slavery is a broad subject that includes different explanations, but this chapter will focus on ancient, biblical, and linguistic topics. Slavery in context requires definitions for a proper understanding. Slavery can be described as intentional, transactional, oppressive, sometimes voluntary, and involuntary. Slavery, in one sense, is "a state of involuntary servitude."[19] Voluntary slavery is perhaps seen mainly in the Old Testament context when a slave loves and willingly stays with their master after the seventh year (e.g., Exod 21:5). The rules about Hebrew slaves are laid out specifically in Exodus (e.g., 21:1-32).

One might also become a slave as a captive or prisoner of war, as is seen frequently in the Old Testament. If not killed, captives of war were likely made subject to their captors as slaves (cf. Exod 1:8-22; Jer 25:1-14).[20] In Paul's day also, individuals and people groups were often publicly enslaved, bought and sold by captors and masters.[21] But other forms of

---

[18] Scriptures reveal voluntary slavery in the Exodus, "But if the slave plainly says, 'I love my master, my wife, and my children; I will not go out as a free man,' then his master shall bring him to God, and he shall bring him to the door or the doorpost. Then his master shall pierce his ear with an awl; and he shall serve him permanently" (Exod 21:5-6; cf. Exod 21:1-11; Duet 15:12-18); Cf., Preface to the English Standard Version (ESV) 2016 text edition, ix-x; cf. LSB, 2021, foreword, III.

[19] Walter A. Elwell, *Evangelical Dictionary of Theology*. 2nd ed. (Grand Rapids, MI: Baker Academic, 2001), 1112.

[20] Cf. Catherine Hezser, *Jewish Slavery in Antiquity*, (Oxford: Oxford University Press, 2009).

[21] Cf. Nordling, "Slavery in Ancient Society," *Philemon*, 39-108. Cf. Nordling, "Theological Implications of Slavery in the New Testament," *Philemon*, 109-139.

slavery were also common. Nordling writes this of ancient slavery's perplexity and its many idiosyncratic forms:

> The ancient evidence of slavery also causes a genuine perplexity at what was—already in antiquity—a complicated and baffling institution. This realization brings us to a problem which should now forthrightly be addressed: in antiquity there were so many different forms of slavery (and, correspondingly, so much potential evidence to consider: literary, papyrological, inscriptional, legal, etc.) that modern interpreters can selectively construct a "preferred view" of ancient slavery that reflects their own preexisting conceits and prejudices. Of course, none of us is free from this predicament. We would not consider Greco-Roman slavery at all, or struggle to come to terms with it accurately, were this institution not so much a part of the world within which Paul wrote his letter to Philemon—or if the correct understanding of slavery (as this institution is depicted in Scripture) were not so essential for any Christian's faithful response to the Gospel still today.[22]

Ancient slavery could be a strange concept to a modern interpreter. For example, Michael Middendorf explains, "While the American experience with slavery is now a distant memory,

---

[22] Nordling, *Philemon*, 42-43.

it is still a painful one. Unfortunately, slavery is put into practice in much of the modern world. Slaves are owned and controlled by their masters unless some form of payment is made to set them free."[23] Payment for freedom from the control of a master is how a slave is commonly freed, whether the slave was purchased, redeemed, or ransomed from by another. Perhaps worldly slave masters, in some circumstances, maliciously declined payment for the freedom of slaves. Then, death was the only escape from worldly and material bondage. The early Christian Church, the Roman Empire, and ancient Israel were more publicly familiar with slaves being bought with a price, owing payment, and legal death as the only means of escape.[24]

Comprehending "slaves" and "servants" as having separate and distinct status is what Paul does intentionally in Romans. For example, Paul uses δοῦλος in the first verse of Romans instead of διάκονος:[25] "Paul, a [δοῦλος] slave of Christ Jesus, a called apostle having been set apart for the Good News of God" (Rom 1:1).[26] The use of the word "slave" instead of "servant" for δοῦλος brings a specific way for readers of the New Testament to comprehend

---

[23] Middendorf, *Romans 1–8*, Concordia Commentary (St. Louis, MO: Concordia Publishing House, 2013), 342.

[24] Cf. Nordling, *Philemon*, 39-108.

[25] In so far as retaining δοῦλος (doulos–*slave*, cf. Rom 1:1; 6:16, 17, 19, 20) and δουλεύω (douleuō–*to be a slave*, cf. Rom 6:6; 7:6, 25; 9:12; 12:11; 14:18; 16:18) instead of διάκονος (diakonos–*servant* of someone, *helper, deacon(ess)*, cf. Rom 13:4; 15:8; 16:1, 27) to keep the context of slavery distinct from servanthood; BDAG, 2nd ed., renders "διάκονος ου, ὁ, ἡ ... *servant* of someone ...," (1979), 184-85, compared to BDAG, 3rd ed., "... one who serves ...," (2000), 230; Cf. Introduction; notes 7-12; For "The Translation of Specialized Terms" such as *doulos* and *ebed*, see Preface to the ESV 2016 text edition, ix-x; And for "The Terminology of Slave," cf. LSB, 2021, foreword, III.

[26] Middendorf, *Romans 1–8*, 57; Again, unless otherwise noted, all English Scripture quotations from the Epistle to the Romans are Middendorf's translation, *Romans 1-8; 9-16*, (2013; 2016), which translates δοῦλος as "slave."

Paul's philological use of slavery (cf. δοῦλος in Nehemiah 1:6,7,10,11 [cf. LXX, LSB, ESV, KJV]).[27] A slave belongs to that master under that lordship. Chris L. De Wet continues, "The slave as one who has no agency outside of the volition of the master; the will of the slave is renounced and totally subservient to that of the slaveholder."[28] Subservience also distinguishes the difference in Paul's use of δοῦλος in Romans 6 rather than διάκονος.

This book attempts to keep δοῦλος as "slave" appropriately. δοῦλος rendered slave is a proper application and hermeneutic of God's Word in the New Testament. Middendorf notes these related terms, "Terms related to 'slave' (δοῦλος, e.g., 1:1; 6:6, 16–17), 'redemption' (ἀπολύτρωσις, 3:24; 8:23), 'to be lord' (κυριεύω, e.g., 6:14; 7:1), 'set free' (ἐλευθερόω, e.g., 6:20, 22; 8:2), and so forth come largely from the background of slavery."[29]

Slavery in the Old Testament

In the Old Testament, slavery language was common among the Prophets and the Psalms. Briefly and notably, the

---

[27] "Syntactically, Paul calls himself *doulos* to make sense of his relationship with Christ, and also to project his authority as an emissary of Christ. The term *diakonos* (servant) of course also features in Paul's writings, but more often than not, it is used to describe service to other members of the Christian community. The term *doulos*, in Pauline literature, was not a synonym for *diakonos*. Why mention this seemingly obvious distinction? Because it may appear problematic for some, perhaps more conservative, readers to consider that one of Christ's primary appellations was that of a slave holder. It is also true that *kyrios* does not always mean 'slaveholder' in New Testament texts." Chris L. De Wet, *Preaching Bondage: John Chrysostom and the Discourse of Slavery in Early Christianity* (University of California Press, 2015), 46-47; See note 128 for further explanation on δοῦλος in the LXX.

[28] De Wet, *Preaching Bondage*, 47.

[29] Middendorf, *Romans 1–8*, 342.

word "עֶבֶד (ebed) as slave"[30] is rendered appropriately in the Old Testament as "slave." Slavery in the context of the Old Testament was ordinary among God's people, as slavery was common in the Greco-Roman period. This is why slavery language was relevant and helpful to God's people in the New Testament. Examining slavery among God's people from the time of the patriarch Abraham will help generate a general comprehension of ancient slavery. Erwin Lueker noted ancient slavery "was practiced among Jews from the time of Abraham, but consciousness of caste is hardly noticeable in patriarchal days; master and slave lived together as members of a household (cf. Gn 15:2–3; 24; 1 Sm 9:5–10; Pr 29:19–21)."[31]

Israel experienced oppressive slavery in Egypt for four hundred thirty years (cf. Exod 1:8-22-12:42).[32] The Israelites were slaves in Egypt until Yahweh freed them (e.g., Ex 20:2; Lev 26:13)."[33] Later, the Babylonian captivity (slavery) lasted for seventy years.[34] Therefore, the examination of slavery in

---

[30] "עֶבֶד n.m. slave, servant ... 1. *slave, servant* of household ..." Francis Brown, William Gesenius, S. R. Driver, and Charles A. Briggs, *A Hebrew and English lexicon of the Old Testament, with an appendix containing the biblical Aramaic* (Oxford: Clarendon, 1951), 713, cf. 713-716. Hereafter, BDB; Cf. "עֶבֶד ... *slave*" William L. Holladay, W. Baumgartner, and Ludwig Koehler, *A Concise Hebrew and Aramaic Lexicon of the Old Testament* (Grand Rapids: William B. Eerdmans Pub, 1971), 262. Hereafter, CHALOT; "עֶבֶד–ebed (713d); from H5647; *slave, servant*: — attendants." NASEC, H5650. This book uses NASEC for Hebrew Strong's references and comparability to BDB and CHALOT; See also, Preface to the English Standard Version (ESV) 2016 text edition, ix-x; cf. Legacy Standard Bible (LSB), 2021, foreword, III.

[31] Erwin Lueker, *Lutheran Cyclopedia*, (St. Louis, MO: Concordia Publishing House, 1975), 720.

[32] Cf. Gen 1 5:13; Acts 7:6; Gal 3:17.

[33] Middendorf, *Romans 1–8*, 342.

[34] For references to the seventy years of Babylonian slavery, cf. 2 Kings 20:17; 24-25 2 Chron 36; Ezra 1:1-2; Jer 25:11, 12; 29:10; Dan 9:2.

the Old Testament connects slavery in the context of Paul's writing to the Romans and the church today.

The Hebrew word עֶבֶד is best translated as "slave" in the context of slavery, even though English translators often render עֶבֶד "servant."[35] Although "servant" at times (cf. Gen 9:25-26, [LSB]) can serve as a proper rendering of עֶבֶד in context, עֶבֶד is another deep study with a broad and narrow range of definitions.

The עֶבֶד – slave of God looks to Him as Master. Yahweh God Almighty is beautifully illustrated as a comparison between a slave and a master. The Psalmist writes, "As the eyes of [עֲבָדִים] slaves look to the hand of their master, as the eyes of a [שִׁפְחָה][36] female slave look to the hand of her mistress, so our eyes look to the LORD our God, till he shows us his mercy."[37] עֶבֶד has been frequently translated as "servant" in English translations, (e.g., Psalm 119:125 [NIV]).[38] Other English versions less often translate עֶבֶד as

---

[35]   Cf. דְּבַע in Genesis 32:10 and compare English translations––LSB, NASB, ESV, KJV. The LSB translates דְּבַע the most as "slave."

[36]   Some older translations (e.g. AV/KJV) use, "תִחְפֵּשׁ n.f. maid, maid-servant ... 1. lit., ... as belonging to a mistress ..." BDB, 1046; "תִחְפֵּשׁ ... female slave, maidservant (not clearly distinguished fm. ʾāmâ) Gn 16:1; humble self-designation 1 S 1:18 . . ." CHALOT, 380; "תִחְפֵּשׁ shiphchah (1046c); from an unused word; maid, maidservant: — female." NASEC, H8198; Compared to some newer translations (e.g. NASB) which use, "מֵכִיתִחְפֵּשׁ: female slave, maidservant (not clearly distinguished fm. ʾāmâ) Gn 16:1; humble self-designation 1 S 1:18." CHALOT, 380; "סִירַעֲשׁ Shaarayim (1045c); from the same as H8179; two cities in Isr.: — maid (2), Shaaraim (3)." NASEC, H8189.

[37]   Psalm 123:2, New International Version (NIV). The New International Version (Grand Rapids, MI: Zondervan, 2011).

[38]   Cf. Psalm 119:17,23,38,49,65,76,84,122,124,125,135,140,176; In comparison to the NIV and other English translations, the LSB notably renders all of these verses with דְּבַע in the Old Testament as slave appropriately, where most English translations do not render these specific verses with דְּבַע as slave, instead, render דְּבַע as servant.

"slave" (cf. Psalm 105:17 in parallel). To better handle the context of slavery, עֶבֶד is most appropriately delivered as "slave" for the reader of all ages in the proper context of slavery.

It would also be pragmatic to define slave and servant, and a few slave–master/mistress words in Hebrew. Master "אָדוֹן (adon) – *lord, master*," and "גְּבֶרֶת (gebereth) – *lady, queen, mistress.*"[39] Comparing the word "slave" in Hebrew consists of a few different words with specific renderings; e.g., עֶבֶד, *slave, servant*, interestingly, שִׁפְחָה *female slave, maidservant*, and "אָמָה (amah)–*female slave, maidservant.*"[40] Perhaps the word "servant" could be helpful at times, yet the word "servant" does not communicate as effectively "slave" for עֶבֶד. "Servant" is often used interchangeably between עֶבֶד, יָלִיד, and נַעַר. This book holds the Hebrew word עֶבֶד appropriately as "slave" in context, just as the Greek word δοῦλος as "slave" in context. Rendering "servant" is perhaps ostensibly overused in English translations for עֶבֶד, conceivably softening and muddling the language for the modern reader.

Slavery in the Old Testament highlights Israel's history of slavery and bondage to Egypt. Slavery in ancient Israel connects to the deliverance from enemies and slavery by

---

39 "וֹדאָ n.m. ... 1. *sg. lord, master* ... 4. יָנֹדֲא יֵנֹדֲא הֹוהְי (*a*) *my Lord Yahweh* ..." BDB, 10-11; "וֹדאָ ... I. (earthly) lord, master ... II. God ... (c) *ʾǎdônây yhwh* my Lord Y." CHALOT, 4; "וֹדאָ adon (10d); from an unused word; lord: — husbands ... יָנֹדֲא Adonay (10d); an emphatic form of H113; *Lord*: — Lord." NASEC, H113, H136; "גְבֶרֶת n.f. 1. *lady, queen* ..." BDB, 150; "גְבֶרֶת ... lady, mistress ... 2. 'lady,' title of queen mother ..." CHALOT, 54; "גְבֶרֶת gebereth (150c); from H1396; *lady, queen, mistress:* — mistress." NASEC, H140.

40 "הָמָא n.f. maid, handmaid ... 1. lit. *maidservant* ..." BDB, 51; "הָמָא ... female slave, maidservant & concubine, orig.: unfree woman ..." CHALOT, 19; "הָמָא amah (51a); of unc. der.; *a maid, handmaid:* — female." NASEC, H519.

Yahweh God.[41] Yahweh God brought Israel "out of the land of Egypt, out of the house of slavery" (Exod 20:2; Deut 5:6; 6:12; 8:12; 13:10, Josh 24:17; Jer. 34:13).[42] Later, Israelite men and women sold as slaves were to be released on the Sabbatical year, remembering Yahweh redeemed the enslaved in Egypt (cf. Duet. 15:12-15). Also, the Babylonian captivity has shown Yahweh's grace and mercy toward Israel in slavery. God gives this grace to Israel in its slavery through Ezra,

> But now for a brief moment grace has been *shown* from Yahweh our God, to leave us an escaped remnant and to give us a peg in His holy place, that our God may enlighten our eyes and give us a little reviving in our slavery. For we are slaves; yet in our slavery our God has not forsaken us, but has extended lovingkindness to us before the kings of Persia, to give us reviving to raise up the house of our God, to restore its waste places, and to give us a wall in Judah and Jerusalem (Ezra 9:8-9; cf. 9:11; Neh 1:4-11; 4-5).

---

[41] Elwell elucidates several claims of slavery in ancient Israel: "Slaves generally performed household duties or labored with the family in the fields. Slaves were acquired by purchase, in payment of debt, by inheritance, by birth, and as prisoners of war. OT instances show a father selling a daughter (Exod. 21:7, Neh. 5:5), a widow selling children (2 Kings 4:1), and people selling themselves (Lev. 25:39; Deut. 15:12-17). A person might be freed from purchase (Lev. 25:48-55), sabbatical year law (Exod. 21:1-11; Deut. 15:12-18), the jubilee year (Lev. 25:8-55), or death of the master (Gen. 15:2) ... Israel as a nation knew bondage in Egypt and thus the exodus experience plays a major role in both OT and the NT." *Evangelical Dictionary of Theology*, 1113; Cf. the Tenth Commandment, "You shall not covet your neighbor's wife or his male slave or his female slave."(Exod 20:17).

[42] Cf. Exod 13:3, 14; Deut 7:8; 13:5; Jdgs 6:8; Mic 6:4.

Slavery in the context of the Old Testament shows slave relationships between earthly rulers, as well as God's lovingkindness and grace toward Israel in captivity, delivering His people as promised. Israel would later be subject to the Roman Empire.

Slavery in the Greco-Roman Age and Modern Slavery

According to scholars, the Roman Empire's slave population is remarkable around the time of Paul. Most historians come to a general estimate of the slave population around the 1st century, which seems accurate in terms of proximity to one another. For example, Walter Scheidel claims,

> I will reckon with six million slaves in a population of sixty million, who thus made up 10 percent of the total population. In this context, the term 'slave' is narrowly defined, excluding free but dependent populations in the provinces. This estimate gives us about two to three million slaves for Italy and three to four million for the provinces.[43]

Other scholars draw from Scheidel's approximately "ten percent"[44] and possibly observe more of the population were

---

[43] Walter Scheidel, "Quantifying the Sources of Slaves in the Early Roman Empire" *Journal of Roman Studies* 87 (1997): 167; See note 44-45 below.

[44] Cf. Scheidel, "Quantifying the Sources of Slaves in the Early Roman Empire," 156-159; Scheidel comments in his notes (16), "This is the only yardstick for the extent of slave-ownership outside the central areas of Roman 'slave society'. Hence, reckoning with a much higher proportion

likely slaves in the Roman Empire during the first century B.C., likely similar in the first century A.D. Sarah Joshel follows, "By the late first century BCE. In Roman Italy, the heartland of the empire, slaves numbered 1 to 1.5 million out of a population of 5 to 6 million, or about 20-30 percent."[45] Ten percent seems to be the lower limit scale for slaves in ancient Rome around the first century. Middendorf notes, "Estimates are that slaves comprised as much as one-third of the population of the Roman Empire."[46] Slaves in the Roman Empire may have been prisoners of war, captives of hired slave captors, born into slavery or abandonment, one who was paying a debt, sold into slavery, and others who sold themselves into slavery.[47]

In comparison to the ancient world of the Greco-Roman period, the approximate number of slaves in 2003 A.D. in the world was an "estimated 27 million men,

---

of slaves in Italy, my estimate of 10 per cent for the Empire as a whole seems rather a lower limit than a reasonable average. The larger the overall share of slaves was, the less likely extraneous sources would have been to meet the demand for replacement slaves: from a methodological point of view, my low estimate serves the useful purpose of making it more difficult for me to argue my case for a high incidence of natural reproduction." Ibid., 116.

[45] Sandra Joshel, *Slavery in the Roman World* (Cambridge: Cambridge University Press, 2010), 8; Cf. Walter Scheidel, "Quantifying the Sources of Slaves in the Early Roman Empire" *Journal of Roman Studies* 87: (1997), 155-169; Many scholars seem to draw from Walter Scheidel, whose research appears helpful in slavery population from the Greco-Roman era and the first century AD Roman Empire.; Cf. Scheidel, "Human Mobility in Roman Italy, II: The Slave Population" *The Journal of Roman Studies*, 95 (2005), 64-79; James S. Jeffers, *The Greco-Roman World Of the New Testament: Exploring the Background of Early Christianity* (Downers Grove, IL: InterVarsity Press, 1999), 221; Peter Hunt, *Ancient Greek and Roman Slavery* (Hoboken, NJ: Wiley-Blackwell, 2018), 43.

[46] Middendorf, *Romans 1–8*, 342.

[47] Cf. Jeffers, *The Greco-Roman World Of the New Testament*, 222.

women, and children in the world who are enslaved—physically confined or restrained and forced to work, or controlled through violence, or in some way treated as property."[48] It is estimated as of 2017, "global estimates of modern slavery estimates that 40.3 million individuals were living in modern slavery ... exploited for the purpose of sexual exploitation, forced labor, forced marriage, domestic servitude, and forced criminality."[49] The modern American slavery population in 2003 A.D. was estimated, "according to Kevin Bales ... between 100,000 and 150,000 slaves in the U.S. today."[50] Disturbingly, according to the 2017 A.D. estimations, "1.9 million men, women, and children were living in modern slavery in the Americas."[51] Most recently, from a study in 2023, the estimate of modern slavery is 50 million people enslaved globally.[52]

According to these estimates, the Roman Empire around the 1st century A.D. exceeds modern slavery in America. Slavery is not a thing of the past only, or an institution that can be solely reduced to America's participation in the African slave trade. Notably, slavery in Paul's day was evident and vast in the Roman Empire. Scrutinizing the slave population is an investigative way to appreciate slavery in the context of the New Testament era and critique Paul's theological thought and slavery language.

---

[48] Andrew Cockburn, "21st-Century Slaves," *National Geographic*, 204, no. 9 (September 2003): 2-3.

[49] "Resource Downloads" Global Slavery Index, accessed 05/06/2022, https://www.globalslaveryindex.org/resources/downloads/. Hereafter "RD" GSI.

[50] Cockburn, "21st-Century Slaves," 7-12.

[51] "RD" GSI, accessed 05/06/2022, https://www.globalslaveryindex.org/resources/downloads/.

[52] Ibid., accessed 01/26/2023, https://www.walkfree.org/global-slavery-index/downloads/; https://cdn.walkfree.org/content/uploads/2023/05/17114737/Global-Slavery-Index-2023.pdf.

Slavery in the New Testament

Paul asserts, "There is neither Jew nor Greek, there is neither slave nor free, there is no male and female, for you are all one in Christ Jesus" (Gal 3:28).[53] All are one in Christ's Kingdom. The slave in Gal 3:28 is the slave of man in the worldly sense. Yet, no matter the ethnicity or gender or status, slaves in Christ in Gal 3:28 are one in Christ's Kingdom, in Paul's day and today. Kerr writes of the early church and the worldly institution of slavery,

> The early church did not attack slavery as an institution. It did, however, reorder the relationship of slave and masters (Philem.), indicate that in God's sight there was neither 'slave nor free' (Gal. 3:28), and state that both were accountable to God (Eph. 6:5-9). The interpersonal relationship was recast in terms of the character of Christ and his kingdom.[54]

This influenced how a Christian viewed being bound to another in Christ and, even, a slave relationship with God.

One might view slavery by the world's standards only and misrepresent the discernment of unity and oneness in Christ alongside one's ethnicity, callings, position, gender, and perhaps a liberal position on equality. Although the reader may be influenced by post-Enlightenment thought, Nordling writes, "Paul would almost certainly not have held

---

[53] Translation by Andrew Das, *Galatians*, ed. Dean O. Wenthe, Concordia Commentary (Saint Louis, MO: Concordia Publishing House, 2014). Unless otherwise noted, Paul's letter to the Galatians in this book is translated by Das.

[54] Elwell, 1113.

post-Enlightenment conceptions of equality, including the common (mis)understanding of many modern Americans and western Europeans today as they ponder a passage like Gal 3:28."[55] Tolerating slavery as a pre-existing institution of the Roman Empire is the consistent teaching of Paul. All are one in Christ, even Christian slaves under a master's rule. Nordling writes about the proper understanding of Galatians 3:28,

> A proper understanding of Gal 3:28 distinguishes those obligations under the Law that have been nullified for all who are justified by faith in Christ from those kinds of obligations that remain in effect for Christians until the return of Christ ... Freedom in Christ, however, is not license—that is, the mistaken idea that Jesus liberates us to be "all that we can be," do whatever we please, or even transgress God's Law by violating Scripture's clear directives. Indeed, St. Paul writes at length about how Christians are in fact dead to sin and alive to God in Christ Jesus (e.g., Rom 6:11–23; Gal 5:16–26).[56]

A Christian master and slave are both described as without distinction among the children of God. Lueker wrote, "Christianity did not require masters to release their servants (cf. Eph 6:5-9) but invited all to be children of God, without [social distinction] (1 Co 7:21-22; Gl 3:28; Cl 3:11;

---

[55]   Nordling, *Philemon*, 61.

[56]   Ibid., 62.

Phmn 10, 16)."[57] Slavery in a Christian context does not categorize a difference in status as children of God, but unity in Christ as Christians, whether master or slave or non-slave.

Slavery as Vocation

As will be discussed in chapters to come, a Christian is called to faith in Baptism, freed from sin, and bound to serve God and neighbor in Christ's righteousness. The slave or free man is bound and called to righteousness and sanctification (*holiness*) under grace in Christ, and is not under the Law of sin and death (cf. Rom 8:2; 6:14, 15, 19, 22).

Most Americans would not categorize a slave as a vocation or calling in sanctified Christian living. Yet a Christian slave could love a neighbor within their bondage through freedom in Christ in various relational situations or vocations. John Nordling writes of slavery as a vocation in the New Testament, "The NT presents slavery as a vocation in which typical Christians could honorably serve God, their master, and many others in ancient society."[58] Vocation is a calling from God in Christ, who loves and serves others as well as honoring God. As a result, a Christian may understand callings in the world in slavery terms without difficulty. Slave as a vocation in the context of Paul's time would be extremely helpful in comprehending what he says about slavery to God and righteousness in Romans 6.

If a Christian is a slave of God in Christ and called to love, the Christian is, in a sense, a slave in vocation under grace and subject to Master Jesus Christ. In a thoughtful perspective of vocation and slavery, Gene Veith highlights

---

[57]   Lueker, *Lutheran Cyclopedia*, 720.
[58]   Nordling, *Philemon*, 43.

an insightful view of *otium*–leisure and *negotium*–busy-ness in the preceding article (see note 59): Veith also mentions,

> Some Christians argued that being a slave *is* a vocation, confusing the Greco-Roman institution cited in the New Testament with the slavery of the new world, which cosigned a whole race to slavery with no provision for individual callings ... After all, the whole point of vocation is that *God* is the one who is working through human beings, as they love and serve each other.[59]

God works in and through his people bound to Christ and his righteousness. Perhaps vocation looks like slavery in the world under grace. Nordling writes,

> We propose that, in the main, *the relationship between master and slaves in the NT and between Christians and persons of greater or less station in the world (as Luther articulated in his doctrine of vocation) is essentially the same.* Let one simple, yet telling, example suffice: substitute "employees" and "bosses" for δοῦλοι ("slaves") and κύριοι ("masters"), respectively, and there remains still today—long after the legal abolishment of slavery in modern democratic societies—essentially the same relationship as obtained long ago in the congregational assemblies in

---

[59] Gene Veith, *Slavery vs. Vocation,* https://www.patheos.com/blogs/geneveith/2021/10/vocation-vs-slavery/?utm_medium=email&utm_source=BRSS&utm_campaign=Evangelical&utm_content=247.

the NT: Slaves [οἱ δοῦλοι], be obedient to your masters according to the flesh [ὑπακούετε τοῖς κατὰ σάρκα κυρίοις] with fear and trembling in sincerity of your heart, just as [you are obedient] to Christ [ὡς τῷ Χριστῷ]––not just service for the sake of appearance, as if you are merely trying to please men, but as slaves of Christ [ὡς δοῦλοι Χριστοῦ], doing [ποιοῦντες] the will of God from your heart, wholeheartedly rendering service as to the Lord [δουλεύοντες ὡς τῷ κυρίῳ], not to men. (Eph 6:5-7; cf. Col 3:22-25) *Let modern Christians see themselves in this picture, then, and not simply dismiss such passages of God's Word as outmoded relics of an earlier age.*[60]

The context of slavery as vocation carries us forward to a theological perspective. A slave to God and righteousness renders service to Yahweh in serving their neighbor in their stations in life. The slave of Christ is delivered by grace and subject to Master Jesus Christ under grace. Nordling argues for the need to study slavery as a vocation,

Slavery should be studied by Christians yet today on account of its pertinence to vocation––that is, to one's life "in Christ" amid the varied circumstances wherein God has set each Christian in this world to be faithful. The sanctified life of a Christian, then, consists not only in

---

a freedom by which Christ sets one free
(e.g., Gal 5:1, 13) but also in being all but
a slave to others among whom God has
set one to be of service (e.g., Gal 5:13;
Rom 6:16, 18; 1 Cor 9:19). Naturally, the
"metaphorical nature" of biblical slavery
is evident in such discussion, yet not so
metaphorical as to obscure the essentially
servile nature of Christianity itself when
carefully considered.[61]

Slavery is a symbolic and literal way to describe the
Christian as belonging to Christ. In fact, slavery is an
undeniable biblical truth one way or the other. Slavery has
an odd and bitter ring to the ears and is hesitantly spoken,
and yet, it is what Paul uses to teach that all people are
either condemned and enslaved to sin or bound to Christ.
Middendorf comments on the harshness of the sound of
slavery, "As harsh as it may sound to human ears in a society
which so often values individualism, personal choice, and
liberty above all, there is, in reality, no alternative to slavery."[62]

Conclusion

Many considerations are too vast on the topic and
context of slavery, so this chapter identified only a few
different types of slavery. Nordling observes the vastness
and complexity of slavery in the ancient era in both positive
and negative senses,

---

[61] Nordling, "Slave to God, Slaves to One Another," *Concordia Theological Quarterly* 80, no. 3-4 (July/October 2016): 232.

[62] Middendorf, *Romans 1–8*, 504.

Because the evidence suggests that types of slavery existed in ancient times that were socially constructive as well as types that were destructive. An understanding of the more complex forms of slavery operative in ancient times will enable modern Christians to consider more accurately the kind of slavery that St. Paul himself would have encountered within the Christian assemblies of his day—within Philemon's house congregation.[63]

Although there is much more to slavery in the context of the Greco-Roman period, Paul uses it to help Christians identify slavery to sin and slavery to God. In the background, Old Testament slavery is helpful to see Israel's relationship to Yahweh, such as deliverance from slavery in the land of Egypt, where Israel was enslaved for over 400 years, and from the Babylonian captivity. In Paul's day, "a slave could have been 'legally dead' no debts to pay back later … extension of masters body."[64]

In a spiritual sense, Paul then asserts that one is born sinful and, therefore, a slave to sin. One is reborn through Baptism, thus paid for, freed, and a slave to God in Christ. The slavery to sin mankind suffers cannot free itself from unless redeemed and declared righteous through faith in Jesus Christ. However, being dead to sin and alive in Christ Jesus covers the entire chapter in Romans 6. The next chapter explores spiritual deadness and slavery to sin and death.

---

[63]   Nordling, *Philemon*, 43.
[64]   Ibid., 43, 44.

The Crucifixion (1523–24), Oil Painting/
Wood by Matthias Grünewald

Two

Spiritual Slavery to Sin

The previous chapter observed the context of earthly slavery in the Greco-Roman era and ancient Israel. As temporal slavery was public among those who lived in the Roman Empire, so an eternal spiritual slavery was widespread and, in fact, common to all. Contemporarily, spiritual slavery is still universal among the entire world. The Bible speaks of this evil spiritual slavery to sin, which has eternal, deadly consequences. In short, sinners are spiritually dead and in slavery to sin.

This chapter primarily examines slavery as a spiritual condition that all people are born into and live out under the dominion of sin. Mankind is under the "Law of sin and death" (Rom 8:2), inherited from the fall of Adam. All people are conceived and born into sin——spiritual slavery to sin and death. From conception to death, "All sinned and are lacking the glory of God" (Rom 3:23). Therefore, "no one does good" (Rom 3:12), and there is not a righteous man on earth born of the flesh who fears and loves God.[65] Instead, slaves to sin are forever captive to fear of death. Hebrews describes "those who through fear of death were subject to slavery all their lives" (Heb 2:15, cf. Rom 8:15).

All sinners are eternally bound by the debt payment of sin for rebellion to God ever since the Fall of man into sin in the Garden (cf. Gen 3).[66] The *Augsburg Confession* states how the fall of Adam resulted in the fall of man and how man is born without the fear of God:

> Likewise, they teach that since the fall of Adam all human beings who are propagated according to nature are born in sin, that is, without fear of God, without trust in God, and with concupiscence.[67]

Spiritual slavery to sin rightly describes how sinners are under the dominion and lordship of sin and powerless over hell and eternal death—"the second death" (Rev 2:11; 20:6, 14; 21:8).[68] Johann Gerhard's examination of hell described hell as slavery, "Hell is called 'captivity' (Ps. 68:18; Eph. 4:8)."[69] In other words, slaves of sin are hell-

---

[65]   Cf. Psalm 14:1-3; 51:1-5; 53:3; Eccl 7:20; John 3:6; Rom 3:9-19, 23. Isaiah writes, "All of us like sheep have gone astray, Each of us has turned to his own way" (Is 53:6).

[66]   Paul writes all sin came through one man, Adam, "Therefore, just as through one man sin entered into the world, and death through sin, and so death spread to all men, because all sinned" (Rom 5:12; cf. vv. 12-21; 1 Cor 15:21-22).

[67]   Robert Kolb, and Timothy J. Wengert, eds. *The Book of Concord: The Confessions of the Evangelical Lutheran Church* (Minneapolis, MN: Fortress Press, 2000), 37, 39. Hereafter, Kolb. *AC* II.1-2; Cf. *Ap* II; *SA* III; *FC Ep* I; *FC SD* I..

[68]   Johann Gerhard, *On the End of the World and Hell*, Theological Commonplaces (St. Louis, Mo: Concordia Publishing House, 2021), 167.

[69]   Gerhard, *On the End of the World and Hell*, Theological Commonplaces, 181.

bound (*slaves of God in Christ are heaven-bound*). The Lutheran Confessions speak further of the slavery to the devil and evil,

> Although the scholastics trivialize both sin and its penalty when they teach that individuals by their own power are capable of keeping the commandments of God, Genesis describes a different penalty imposed on account of original sin. For their human nature was not only subjected to death and other bodily ills, but also to the reign of the devil. There this horrible sentence is pronounced [Gen. 3:15*]: "I will put enmity between you and the woman, and between your offspring and hers." The deficiency and concupiscence are both penalty and sin. Death and other bodily ills, together with the tyranny of the devil, are penalties in the proper sense. For human nature is enslaved and held captive by the devil, who deceives it with ungodly opinions and errors and incites it to all sorts of sins. However, just as the devil is not conquered without Christ's help, so we, by our own powers, are unable to free ourselves from that slavery. World history itself shows how great is the strength of the devil's rule. Blasphemy and wicked teachings fill the world, and in these bonds the devil holds enthralled those who are wise and righteous in the eyes of the world.[70]

---

[70] Kolb, *The Book of Concord: The Confessions of the Evangelical Lutheran Church*, 119. *Apology* II.46-49.

Human nature is corrupt and godless because of original sin, resulting in being a slave of Satan and his works of lawlessness. Unless repentant faith in Christ is given to the slave to sin, the Second Death (cf. Rev 20:14; 21:8) is the culmination of eternal separation from God's love and mercy in Christ. The slave to sin will remain under the wrath of God in eternal "outer darkness" (Matt 25:30) and suffering. Spiritual slavery to sin results in an eternal condemnation the entire world suffers.

Slavery to sin is an eternal spiritual condition and yet has physical effects—a spiritually dead state of the physical body and soul. The slave to sin is a whole "[σῶμα] body of sin"[71] (Rom 6:6). Middendorf notes, "The idea is of the body as controlled and dominated by sin, a point clarified by the clause which follows."[72] A body of sin is "enslaved to sin."[73]

---

[71] "σῶμα ... 'body.'— ① body of a human being or animal ... *b. the living body* ... Because it is subject to sin and death, man's mortal body as τὸ σῶμα τῆς σαρκός (σάρξ 2cα) Col 2:11 is a σῶμα τῆς ἁμαρτίας Ro 6:6." BDAG, 983-84; "σῶμα sōma; of unc. or.; *a body:* — bodies ... (1) slaves ..." NASEC, G4983; Middendorf textual note; "σῶμα is not the opposite of the immaterial "spirit" or "soul" in a Platonic sense, even though Paul does occasionally utilize that terminology (e.g., 1 Thess 5:23)." *Romans 1–8*, 448.

[72] Middendorf, *Romans 1–8*, 449.

[73] Slavery to sin is a "body of sin" (Rom 6:6; cf. 7:24), dying in the deadness of sin where death reigns (Rom 5:21; cf. 5:12, 14), and evil is present (Rom 7:21). A slave to sin is trafficked under sin (7:14; cf. Rom 3:9; Gal 3:22), under "the curse of the Law" (Gal 3:13; cf. Rom 2:12; 3:19; 6:14, 15), and "the authority of darkness" (Col 1:13). A slave to sin is captive under the evil one, the "spiritual forces of wickedness in the heavenly places" (Eph 6:12; cf. 2:2) and "the authority of Satan" (Acts 26:18; cf.; Heb 2:14; 1 John 5:19), the devil, and truthless father of lies and murderer (John 8:44). The *Confessio Augustana* states: "Concerning the cause of sin it is taught among us that although almighty God has created and preserves all of nature, nevertheless the perverted will causes sin in all those who are evil and despise God. This, then, is the will of the devil and of all the ungodly. As soon as God withdrew his hand, it turned from

Slavery to sin is an irreversible consequence no man can pay to cancel or redeem. Scripture states, "Truly, no man can redeem *his* brother; He cannot give to God a ransom for him——For the redemption price for their soul is costly, And it ceases forever" (Psalm 49:7-8). Therefore, slavery to sin is a grave and deadly problem for which the payment of death is owed forever. Only God can ransom the slave to sin, as the next chapter will navigate. Tragically, unrepentant and faithless sinners remain ungodly and condemned to death under the Law of sin and death.

Sin and death rule and lord over the slave to sin. James Dunn observes, "*ἤτοι ἁμαρτίας εἰς θάνατον*, 'whether of sin to death' [Rom 6:16]. This is the only instance of *ἤτοι* in NT. 'Sin' continues to be personified as the power which exercises effective rule over those whose lives are confined within this age ... As in 5:21 death is the final and most complete expression of sins power over man."[74] Paul connects the Law and the power of sin; "the sting of death is sin, and the power of sin is the [Law]" (1 Cor 15:56). Therefore Paul writes that "as many as sinned in [the] Law, they will be judged through [the] Law" (Rom 2:12; cf. 6:14, 15). Sin and death reign (cf. Rom 5:17, 21) for slaves to sin under the Law and in their mortal bodies (cf. Rom 6:12; 8:2, 11). Sinners cannot stop or thwart the lordship and power of sin. Richard Lenski commented,

> In [Rom.] 5:17 'the death reigned,' here [Rom. 6:12] Paul says, 'Let not the sin reign,' meaning 'the death' and 'the sin' as

---

God to malice, as Christ says (John 8[:44*]): "When [the devil] lies, he speaks according to his own nature." Kolb, *The Book of Concord*, 52. *AC* XIX.

[74] James Dunn, *Romans 1-8*, Word Biblical Commentary, vol. 38A (Grand Rapids, MI: Zondervan, 1988), 342.

> powers ... Now it would be useless to tell
> sinners not to let this powerful king, sin,
> reign over them, whether in their mortal
> bodies or in the rest of their being; sinners
> could not prevent this sin's reigning over
> them.[75]

The curse of sin scourges the slave to sin, completely paralyzing the sinner from preventing or averting the reign of sin and death over mankind. Apart from Christ, sin is lord over the sinner. The slave to sin remains a slave who produces only evil deeds and is forever dead in sins and trespasses (cf. Eph 2:1, 5).[76]

Only Bad Fruit

The slave to sin produces nothing good, godly, or righteous. Instead, the slave to sin always yields to ungodliness and unrighteousness. "As long as you were slaves of sin, you were free [in regard] to righteousness" (Rom 6:20). Freedom from righteousness never yields good fruit. Slavery to sin is unrighteousness that always leads to sin and death.[77] Paul

---

[75] Richard C. H. Lenski, *Interpretation of St Paul's Epistle to the Romans.* (Minneapolis, MN: Augsburg Fortress, 2008), 411.

[76] "And you were dead in your transgressions and sins, in which you formerly walked according to the course of this world, according to the ruler of the power of the air, the spirit that is now working in the sons of disobedience, among whom we all also formerly conducted ourselves in the lusts of our flesh, doing the desires of the flesh and of the mind, and were by nature children of wrath, even as the rest" (Eph 2:1-3).

[77] "Paul introduces another metaphor in 6:21, that of 'fruit' (καρπός). It is a negative image in 6:21, but expressed positively in 6:22 in a manner comparable to 'the fruit of the Spirit' in Gal 5:22–23." Middendorf, *Romans 1–8*, 506.

writes, "Therefore what fruit were you having at that time? Upon which things you are now ashamed, for the outcome of those things is death" (Rom 6:21; cf. 7:5). Freedom from righteousness is not actually freedom at all; but slavery to sin and unrighteousness. Middendorf explains freedom from righteousness,

> In 6:20, Paul speaks of the "before" state—slavery to sin—in terms comparable to 6:17 and 6:19: "indeed, for as long as you were slaves of sin, you were free [in regard] to righteousness." Of course, this was not really freedom, but slavery to unrighteousness (cf. 6:13). More significantly, it was being "free" in the sense of separation from God and exclusion from the reign of his grace. It was living apart from or "independent" (BDAG, s.v., ἐλεύθερος, 2) of righteousness (see the textual note). This echoes Paul's quotation of Eccl 7:20 in Rom 3:10: "there is not a righteous person, not even one." Paul ends 6:21 by asserting what he demonstrated throughout 1:18–3:20 and will state in 6:22–23. In contrast to the "outcome" (τέλος) of "being enslaved to God" (6:22), an existence free from righteousness can only result in "death" (6:23).[78]

---

[78] Ibid; Textual note, "6:20 ὅτε γὰρ δοῦλοι ἦτε τῆς ἁμαρτίας—The temporal particle ὅτε serves as a 'marker of a period of time coextensive with another period of time, as long as, while' (BDAG, 2). It is followed by the imperfect of εἰμί. Together they describe a past state of being, 'as long as you were slaves of sin,' the first of two eras." Middendorf, *Romans 1–8*, 491.

Slavery to sin is, therefore, spiritual deadness free of any righteousness.

Indeed, sin and death are fruitless endeavors of godlessness—a bad fruit of death for the slave to sin. Jesus said, "If your eye is bad, your whole body will be full of darkness. If then the light in you is darkness, how great is the darkness!" (Matt 6:23; cf. Luke 11:34). When the eye is bad, it remains in spiritual darkness and slavery to sin. Slavery to unrighteousness is spiritual darkness and death, resulting in bad fruit of eternal death. Middendorf elucidates,

> Jesus also speaks of fruit both positively and negatively and indicates that a change in the tree must take place before good fruit is possible: Either make the tree good and its fruit good, or make the tree bad and its fruit bad; for the tree is known from the fruit.... The good man out of his good treasure brings forth good, and the evil man out of his evil treasure brings forth evil. (Mt 12:33, 35) Paul similarly describes the shameful fruit formerly produced by slaves of sin who used to live apart from righteousness: "Therefore what fruit were you having at that time? Upon which things you are now ashamed, for the outcome of those things is death" (6:21).[79]

Sin only produces more sin and evil, leading to death. Therefore, the bad tree that bears bad fruit is evil, and the slave to sin is part of the bad tree that can only produce sin

---

[79] Ibid.

and evil. So "the evil person out of his evil treasure produces evil, for out of the abundance of the heart his mouth speaks" (Luke 6:45; cf. Matt 12:35; Gen 8:21; Prov 12:20). Sadly, this is the case. Mankind is cursed forever under sin and death due to rebellion against God.

Slavery to sin and death cursed mankind and the world ever since Adam and Eve ate fruit from the forbidden tree in the Garden of Eden (cf. Gen 3).[80] Yahweh God said to Adam that he would die for eating from the tree; he would return to dust.

> By the sweat of your face
> You shall eat bread,
> Till you return to the ground,
> Because from it you were taken;
> For you are dust,
> And to dust you shall return" (Gen 3:19).

All of mankind would return to dust due to rebellion against Yahweh in the Garden. So mankind is enslaved to sin without the power and wisdom of God or His righteousness.[81] Therefore, the slave to sin remains under the Law, dead and bound to death and the devil.

---

[80] "And Yahweh God commanded the man, saying, 'From any tree of the garden you may surely eat; but from the tree of the knowledge of good and evil, you shall not eat from it; for in that day that you eat from it you will surely die ... And the serpent said to the woman, You will not surely die! ... Then the woman saw that the tree was good for food, and that it was a delight to the eyes, that the tree was desirable to make *one* wise, so she took from its fruit and ate; and she gave also to her husband with her, and he ate" (Gen 2:16-17; 3:4, 6; cf. 3:1-12).

[81] Yahweh said to the serpent, "And I will put enmity between you and the woman, and between your seed and her seed; He shall bruise you on the head, and you shall bruise him on the heel" (Gen 3:15). This fulfillment is seen in Jesus Christ, God incarnate, "But when the fullness of time

There is no forgiveness or hope for the slave to sin who rejects Christ and remains dead apart from Christ. There is no good fruit apart from Jesus; there is only bad fruit. For Jesus says,

> As the branch cannot bear fruit from itself unless it abides in the vine, neither can you unless you abide in me. "I am the vine, you are the branches; he who abides in Me and I in him, he bears much fruit, for apart from me you can do nothing" (John 15:4-5).

The slave to sin is always subject to the masters, sin, death, and Satan, and cannot overcome their power. Indeed, the slave to sin hates God, and His Son incarnate. Jesus says, "He who hates Me hates My Father also" (John 15:23). The slave to sin hates Christ and therefore remains dead and faithless, without forgiveness and liable to pay a debt of eternal death.

The Payment of Sin is Death

Sin has a price, and the payment is death for sinners under the Law (Rom 6:14, 15; 8:2). Paul wrote, "For the [οψωνια][82] payment of sin is death" (Rom 6:23; cf. 5:12).

---

came, God sent forth His Son, born of a woman, born under Law" (Gal 4:4). The slave to sin has no hope for freedom from slavery to sin but Christ alone, the promised offspring/seed of the woman (cf. Gen 3:15). Christ would bring hope, salvation, and freedom from sin for all sinners expounded upon in the next chapter, the promise and deliverance from spiritual slavery to sin in Christ.

[82] "6:23 τὰ γὰρ ὀψώνια—The picture now shifts from slavery to military and/or fiscal language." Middendorf, *Romans 1–8*, 492; "ὀψώνιον, ου, τό ... ① pay, wages ... ⓑ in imagery of Christians as soldiers (on the

Payment of eternal death is owed to God. Yahweh's wrath and destruction remain on unrepentant sinners.[83] Those without godly repentance (cf. 2 Cor 7:9-11) perish eternally––"unless you repent, you will all likewise perish"[84] (Luke 13:3, 5). There is no escape for the slave to sin! Slaves to

---

Christian life as military service s. πανοπλία 2), whose wages are paid by the heavenly general: ἀρέσκετε ᾧ στρατεύεσθε, ἀφ' οὗ καὶ τὰ ὀψώνια κομίζεσθε IPol 6:2.—The military viewpoint seems to pass over into a more general one in λαβὼν ὀψώνιον πρὸς τὴν ὑμῶν διακονίαν accepting support so that I might serve you 2 Cor 11:8 ... Ro 6:23 is still further fr. the military scene, and it is prob. better to class it under the foll ... ② compensation (IPriene 121, 34 [I B.C.], public services χωρὶς ὀψωνίων; 109, 94; 106 [II B.C.] ἄτερ ὀψωνίου) τὰ ὀψώνια τ. ἁμαρτίας θάνατος the compensation paid by sin (for services rendered to it) is death Ro 6:23 ...." BDAG, 747; οψωνια, "ὀψώνιον opsōnion; from the same as G3795 and G5608; provisions, wages: — expense" NASEC, G3800.

[83] God's Word of warning and strange alien work of destruction for unrepentant scoffers. One can see Yahweh's "unusual [רז,רוז–*foreign, strange*] work ... His exceptional [יִתְכַנ–*alien*] labor ... Of complete destruction [הֲלָכְ־יְכֹ]" (Isa 28:21, 22); "I. [רוז] vb. be a stranger . . .וַהַשַׁעַמ רָז Is 28²¹ *his work is foreign* (as if dealing with enemies) ..." BDB, 266; "ורז ... turn away from ..." CHALOT, 87; "רוז zur (266b); a prim. root; *to be a stranger:* — adulteress." NASEC, H2114a; "יִתְכַנ adj. foreign, alien . . . וְתִדְבֹעַ הֲיַ יִתְכַנ Is 28²¹ *strange is his task !*" BDB, 648-49; "יִתְכַנ foreign, strange ... 2. strange, alien ... odd, surpassing Is 28₂₁." CHALOT, 239; "יִתְכַנ nokri (648d); from the same as H5235b; foreign, alien: — adulteress." NASEC, H5237; Paul said to those in the synagogue on the Sabbath with Barnabas in Pisidia, "Therefore watch out, so that the thing spoken of the Prophets may not come upon you: LOOK YOU SCOFFERS, AND MARVEL, AND PERISH; FOR I AM ACCOMPLISHING A WORK IN YOUR DAYS, A WORK THAT YOU WILL NEVER BELIEVE, THOUGH SOMEONE SHOULD RECOUNT IT TO YOU" (Acts 13:40-41; cf. Hab 1:5).

[84] Jesus speaks of repentance as He said to some in the crowd inquiring about the Galileans' blood Pilate mixed with their sacrifices, "Do you think that these Galileans were *greater* sinners than all *other* Galileans because they suffered these things? "I tell you, no, but unless you repent, you will all likewise perish. "Or do you think that those eighteen on whom the tower fell and killed them were *worse* offenders than all the men who live in Jerusalem? "I tell you, no, but unless you repent, you

sin are in the grasp of sin's infinite evil and ugliness. Sin separates mankind from God. Gerhard wrote, "Sin is an infinite evil because it offends God, who is the infinite good. It separates from God, who is the unique and highest good. Therefore it deserves infinite—that is, eternal—punishment. Rom. 6:23: 'The wages of sin is death'—not only temporal but also eternal, as the contrast show."[85] Sin deserves eternal punishment. No power of man or human will can ever satisfy God for redemption from sin and eternal death.

Since death is the payment due for sin, the slave to sin remains evil and forever judged as ungodly. It is impossible for man to save and redeem himself or another from sin and death. The *Formula of Concord* explains, "For because our nature, corrupted by sin, deserves God's wrath and condemnation, God owes us neither his Word nor Spirit nor grace ... For it is not unjust when they are punished and receive the 'wages of sin' [Rom. 6:23]."[86] Since this debt and wages of sin is eternal death, a death payment is owed to God for disobedience. Therefore, sin is a problem, and mankind is inadequate to redeem any soul from death.

Whatever the slave to sin does always leads to death. Paul writes, "Do you not understand that to whom[ever] you present yourselves [as] slaves for obedience, you are slaves to whom[ever] you respond, whether of sin leading to death or of responsiveness to God leading to righteousness?" (Rom 6:16). Slaves who respond to sin are slaves of sin and death.

---

will all likewise perish." (Luke 13:2-5; cf. Matt 11:20; 25:412-46; Rev 9:20, 21; 16).

[85] Gerhard, 202.

[86] Kolb, 650. *FC SD*, Article XI.60-61.

The Slave to Sin Commits Sin

The severity of slavery to sin inevitably results in the sinner committing sinful acts. In John's Gospel, Jesus describes those who are slaves to sin. "Jesus said to the Jews, 'Truly, truly, I say to you, everyone who commits sin is a slave of sin'" (John 8:34; cf. 1 John 3:4-10). Truly slaves to sin cannot help but commit sin since they are in bondage under the rule and power of Satan. Therefore, John writes, "The one who does sin is of the devil, because the devil sins from the beginning" (1 John 3:8; cf. John 8:44). Slaves of sin do what the devil does; sinners commit sin. Paul also teaches that all are under sin (Rom 3:9; 7:14; Gal 3:22) and that sin has dominion as ruler and master. According to Paul's teaching, one also learns that the Law condemns.

Since "the payment of sin is death" (Rom 6:23), the inescapable payment of death has to be settled. Jesus said, "Therefore I said to you that you will die in your sins. For unless you believe that I am *He*, you will die in your sins" (John 8:24). The one who rejects the grace of God in Christ dies an eternal death as a slave to sin. Martin Franzmann wrote,

> What the Christian knows, but is always tempted to forget is, is the hard fact that we cannot take sin or leave it. Once we take sin, sin has taken us; for sinning is always at bottom rebellion against God and removes us from Him. Removed from Him, we return inevitably to the domination of sin. Paul's word is an echo of Jesus' saying: "Every one who commits sin is a slave to sin" (John 8:34). Freedom to sin

is therefore merely a passport to slavery and a consignment to death. The alternative to this slavery is a slavery too. Paul calls it, rather strangely, a slavery to obedience.[87]

The slave to sin is obedient to sin under the Law and the lordship of sin, death, and Satan. Condemnation is an actual true death without Christ, as death is the inescapable and inevitable reality for all enslaved to sin.

Slavery to Impurity and Lawlessness

Slavery to sin equals death. And death is the sum of sin. And Paul writes, "The sting of death is sin, and the power of sin is the law" (I Cor 15:56). Slaves to sin present bodily members to uncleanness, impurity, and lawless deeds. Paul writes, "You presented your bodily members [as] slavish to [ἀκαθαρσίᾳ][88] impurity and to a [ἀνομίᾳ] [89] lawless mindset leading to lawless behavior" (Rom 6:19; cf. 1 John 5:16). A slave to ἀκαθαρσίᾳ–impurity is already impure in sinful action and is unclean. And a slave to ἀνομίᾳ–lawlessness forever works lawless deeds. Impurity and a "lawless mindset" are indeed unrighteousness. Paul describes this in the first chapter of Romans,

---

[87] Martin Franzmann, *Romans*, Concordia Commentary (St. Louis, MO: Concordia Publishing House, 1968), 116-17.

[88] "ἀκαθαρσία, ας, ἡ ... in var. senses of something that is not clean ... ② fig. a state of moral corruption ..." BDAG, 34; "ἀκαθαρσία akatharsia; from G169; *uncleanness:* — impurity." NASEC, G167.

[89] "ἀνομία, ας, ἡ ... ① state or condition of being disposed to what is lawless, *lawlessness*, opp. δικαιοσύνη (Hdt. 1, 96; X., Mem. 1, 2, 24 ἀνομίᾳ μᾶλλον ἢ δικαιοσύνῃ χρώμενοι) Ro 6:19a; 2 Cor 6:14; BDAG, 85; "ἀνομία anomia; from G459; *lawlessness:* — lawless deed" Cf. NASEC, G458.

> Having become filled up with every
> unrighteousness, wickedness, greediness,
> [and] evil; full of envy, murder, strife,
> deceit, [and] meanness; [they are] gossipers,
> slanderers, God-haters, arrogant, puffed up,
> boastful, [and] inventors of evil; [they are]
> disobedient to parents, lacking common
> sense, disloyal, without affection, and
> merciless; such ones who, even though they
> recognize the righteous decree of God that
> the ones who practice things like these are
> deserving of death, not only do them, but
> also think well of those who practice [them]
> (Rom 1:29-32).

Slaves to sin are filled with unrighteousness and practice unrighteousness. God's holy Law condemns impurity and lawlessness. Yet the Law and commandment are "holy and righteous and good" (Rom 7:12). Paul explains how the good Law exposes sin,

> Therefore did that which is good become
> death for me? May it never come to be! But
> sin, in order that sin might be exposed, was
> accomplishing death [in] me through the
> Good, so that, through the commandment,
> sin might come to be exceedingly sinful.
> For we understand that the Law is Spiritual,
> but I am fleshly, having been sold and still
> under sin" (Rom 7:13, 14; cf. Rom 3:9;
> Gal 4:3).[90]

---

[90] "Since the context of Ac 23:29 ἐγκαλούμενον περὶ ζητημάτων τοῦ νόμου αὐτῶν points to the intimate connection between belief, cult, and

Even though the Law is good, the Law also exposes sin, and the slave to sin remains under the Law.

Spiritual slavery to sin is evil. Death has dominion over all mankind enslaved to sin (cf. Rom 6:6, 9, 14). The spiritually dead, the "παλαιὸς ἡμῶν ἄνθρωπος–our old self"[91] (Rom 6:6), is where death rules apart from Christ. Paul identifies this as enslavement to sin. Sin reigns in all ἄνθρωπος–mankind who are not under grace. For the one under sin cannot resist the power of sin. Slavery to sin is an inescapable reality, a reality under Law.

---

communal solidarity in Judean tradition, the term νόμος is best rendered with an hendiadys: (charged in matters) relating to their belief and custom; cp. v. ὁ καθ' ὑμᾶς 18:15. Ro 9:31 (CRhyne, Νόμος Δικαιοσύνης and the meaning of Ro 10:4: CBQ 47, '85, 486–99).—Abs., without further qualification ὁ v. Mt 22:36; 23:23; Lk 2:27; J 1:17; Ac 6:13; 7:53; 21:20, 28; Ro 2:15 (τὸ ἔργον τοῦ νόμου the work of the law [=the moral product that the Mosaic code requires] is written in the heart; difft. Diod S 1, 94, 1 v. ἔγγραπτος, s. 1b, above), 18, 20, 23b, 26; 4:15a, 16; 7:1b, 4–7, 12, 14, 16; 8:3f; 1 Cor 15:56; Gal 3:12f, 17, 19, 21a, 24; 5:3, 14; 1 Ti 1:8 (GRudberg, ConNeot 7, '42, 15); Hb 7:19 (s. Windisch, Hdb. exc. ad loc.), 28a; 10:1; cp. Js 2:9 (s. 1b above); μετὰ τὸν v. Hb 7:28b; οἱ ἐν τῷ v. Ro 3:19; κατὰ τὸν v. according to the (Mosaic) law (Jos., Ant. 14, 173; 15, 51 al.; Just., D. 10, 1) J 19:7b; Ac 22:12; 23:3; Hb 7:5; 9:22." BDAG, 677.

[91] παλαιὸς ἡμῶν ἄνθρωπος–old our self/man (cf. Rom 6:6); "παλαιός, ά, όν ... ① pert. to being in existence for a long time, old ... ② pert. to that which is obsolete or inferior because of being old, old, obsolete fig. ὁ π. ἄνθρωπος the old (i.e. earlier, unregenerate) person or self (ἄνθρωπος 5b) Ro 6:6; Eph 4:22; Col 3:9." BDAG, 751; "ἄνθρωπος, ου, ὁ ... 'human being, man, person'... ① a person of either sex, w. focus on participation in the human race, a human being ... ⑤ a being in conflict at a transcendent level ... ⓓ from another viewpoint, w. contrast of παλαιὸς and καινὸς (νέος) ἄ. Ro 6:6; Eph 4:22, 24; Col 3:9 (cp. Dg 2:1; Jesus as καινὸς ἄ. IEph 20:1 is the new being, who is really God), or of ὁ ψυχικὸς ἄ. and ὁ πνευματικός ἄ. 1 Cor 2:14f (s. πνευματικός 2αγ). τὸν τέλειον ἄ. GMary 463, 27." BDAG, 81-82; "παλαιός palaios; from G3819; old, ancient: — old." NASEC, G3820.

Instruments for Unrighteousness Under Law

Slavery to sin exhibits itself as becoming an instrument for unrighteousness under the Law. Paul calls for believers to cease those former activities. "And do not continue to present your bodily members to sin [as] instruments of unrighteousness" (Rom 6:13). "Instruments of unrighteousness" implies that the slave to sin presents its bodily members to unrighteousness. The slave to sin is an "ὅπλον–instrument or weapon"[92] of unrighteousness. Therefore, the slave to sin is bound to "ἀδικία–unrighteousness."[93] The flesh and sinful passion always present as unrighteousness, aroused by the Law. Paul writes, "For when we were in [the realm of] the flesh, the passions of the sins, which [passions] were through the Law, were at work in our bodily members with the result that we produced fruit [leading] to death" (Rom 7:5; cf. Col 3:5). The slave to sin produces fruit leading to death which arms, defends, and upholds its master as a slavish instrument of unrighteousness. Whether the slave to sin knows of sin and unrighteousness does not change that the slave to sin remains sinful, serving unrighteousness, sin, death, and Satan in thought, word, and deed (*as opposed to the*

---

[92] "ὅπλον, ου, τό ... ① any instrument one uses to prepare or make ready, tool ὅπλα ἀδικίας *tools of wickedness*, i.e. tools for doing what is wicked Ro 6:13a (cp. Aristot., Pol. 1253a). Opp. ὅπλα δικαιοσύνης vs. 13b. But mng. 2 is also prob.; it is found in all the other pass. of our lit., and specif. in Paul. ② an instrument designed to make ready for military engagement, *weapon*." BDAG, 716; "ὅπλον hoplon; a prim. word; *a tool, implement, weapon:* — armor." NASEC, G3696.

[93] "ἀδικία, ας, ἡ ... ① an act that violates standards of right conduct, *wrongdoing* ... ② the quality of injustice, *unrighteousness, wickedness, injustice* . . . ὅπλα ἀδικίας *weapons of unrighteousness* Ro 6:13. —The gen. is oft. found as in Sem. lang. (cp. 2 Km 3:34; 7:10; Hos 12:8), but also in nonbiblical Gk." BDAG, 20; "ἀδικία adikia; from G94; *injustice, unrighteousness:* — doing wrong." NASEC, G93.

slave of God serving righteousness, life, and Jesus Christ in thought, word, and deed through faith).

The slave to sin is overpowered and seized by the condition of the flesh, that is, the sinful nature, whether knowingly or unknowingly. For the slave to sin, the Law of sin and death controls sinners' desires, and they cannot serve God or be controlled by Christ. The slave to sin is controlled by sin under the Law (*Christ controls the slave to God under grace*). The weapons of unrighteousness are what slaves to sin always have and do. The slave to sin is a bad instrument of unrighteousness under the Law. Sin has dominion as lord over the slave to sin under the Law (cf. Rom 6:14, 15).[94] So, either God is "κυριεύω—lord, master"[95] over the slave under grace, or sin and death have dominion (cf. Rom 6:9, 14) over the one enslaved. In the case of the one enslaved to sin under the Law (cf. Rom 6:14; 15; 7:23, 25; 8:2), sin is lord.[96] The one who sins is under the Law (Rom 6:15) and is a slave to sin and Satan. Martin Luther explains,

---

[94] As for the slave to Christ, in contrast to the slave to sin, Paul writes, "Indeed, sin will not be lord [κυριευσει] of you; for you are not under Law but under grace" (Rom 6:13) Jesus has dominion as Lord over the slave to God and righteousness under grace.

[95] "κυριεύω ... 'to be lord/master of' ① to exercise authority or have control, *rule*, of persons, w. gen. of that over which rule or control is exercised ... ② be master of, dominate, of things that take control of a pers., transf. sense of 1 and likew. w. the gen. (Sextus 41; 363a; Philo, Leg. All. 3, 187 πάθος; TestSim 3:2, Iss 7:7): of the law κυριεύει τοῦ ἀνθρώπου Ro 7:1 (JDerrett, Law in the NT, '70, 461–71). Of sin 6:14. Of death vs. 9.—B. 1319." BDAG, 576; "κυριεύω kurieuō; from G2962; to be lord of, rule: — has jurisdiction over." NASEC, G2961.

[96] "When the Law identifies sin, *the Law also takes man captive to sin and condemns him to death* (see [Rom] 7:1,5,24; 8:2; compare also 3:20; 4:15; 5:12,18,20; 6:14-15,23)." Middendorf, *The "I" in the Storm: A Study of Romans 7* (St. Louis, MO: Concordia Publishing House, 1997), 111; see Middendorf, The "I" in the Storm, 106-129.

From the plain fact, which is evidenced by Scriptures that are neither ambiguous nor obscure, that Satan is by far the most cunning and powerful ruler of this world (as we have said), and as long as he reigns the human will is not free nor under its own control, but is the slave of sin and Satan, and can only will what its master wills. Nor will he permit it to will anything good—though Satan were not in command of it, sin itself, of which man is the slave, would press heavily enough on him to make him unable to will the good.[97]

Thus, the slave to sin is entirely enslaved, body and soul, and not free to turn to God. And so, bound to sin, death, and Satan, the will is bound as a slave and not free.

Conclusion

Elaborated throughout Romans 6, spiritual slavery to sin is slavery to sin and death. The old man is fully enslaved to sin—an unkind, miserable, and unmerciful existence. Sin and death show no mercy. Death reigns and has dominion over the slave to sin. The slave of sin listens and responds to its master. Furthermore, a slave to sin works ungodliness as an instrument of unrighteousness under the curse of

---

[97] Martin Luther, "Bondage of the Will" (1525): vol. 33, 238 in *Luther's Works, American Edition*, vols. 1–30, ed. Jaroslav Pelikan (St. Louis: Concordia, 1955–76); vols. 31–55, ed. Helmut Lehmann (Philadelphia/Minneapolis: Muhlenberg/Fortress, 1957–86); vols. 56–82, ed. Christopher Boyd Brown and Benjamin T. G. Mayes (St. Louis: Concordia, 2009). Hereafter *AE*.

the Law. The slave to sin is free from righteousness. The slave to sin presents itself to the master sin as impure and unrighteous, leading to death as payment for sin is death. Dunn explains the payment of death for sinners, "Paul's characterization of this eternal life as a 'free gift' in contrast the wages of death may be intended to recall similar contrast in [Rom] 4:4—the point being that God owes man nothing; if the talk is to be of something earned, then only death is in view." [98] The slave to sin is, therefore, forever dead in sin.

Mankind owes God death as payment for sin. Death as payment for sin rightly describes the result of slavery to sin. Slavery to sin is a wicked and ungodly rebellion toward God. The psalmist writes, "Transgression declares to the ungodly within his heart; There is no dread of God before his eyes ... But transgressors will be altogether destroyed; The posterity of the wicked will be cut off" (Psalm 36:1, 37:38; cf. Rom 3:18; 5:16). All sinners are condemned forever under the Law of sin and death. Middendorf explains, "Paul describes all people as being under sin, death, and the condemnation of the Law. But Christ's death and resurrection frees people from that slavery in order that they might willingly serve God and one another."[99] This leads into the next chapter. Having been declared righteous from sin, the Christian is transferred from the rule of sin under Law to the reign and kingdom of Christ under grace in faith and Baptism.

---

[98]   Dunn, *Romans 1-8*, vol. 38A, 356-57.
[99]   Middendorf, *Romans 1–8*, 342. To willingly serve as a slave of Christ and His righteousness.

The Resurrection (1510), Woodcut Print by Albrecht Dürer

THREE

FREED FROM SLAVERY TO SIN

This chapter examines Paul's explanation of freedom from slavery to sin in Romans 6. The last chapter discussed how mankind is born sinful and unrighteous, slaves to sin. For all sin and are under the condemnation of the Law, sin, death, and Satan. In contrast, this chapter explains how sinners are freed from slavery to sin and become slaves to God under grace. Having received righteousness on account of Christ Jesus, the sinner is freed from slavery to sin. Christians are no longer condemned, but justified and declared righteous from the judgment of the Law, sin, death, and Satan. Freedom from slavery to sin results from the fact that all sin has been paid for on account of Christ Jesus. Those Baptized into Jesus Christ are created anew through faith, resurrected from the dead with Christ to life everlasting.

The slave to sin is born a slave because of original sin, the result of Adam and Eve's rebellion against God in the garden. The slave to God is freed from all the consequences of sin, original and actual, through the crucified and risen

Redeemer and Savior of the sinful world, Jesus Christ. Forgiveness of sins and justification from sin gives sinners declared righteousness and redemption from sin to all who believe and are Baptized. Freedom from slavery to sin only exists in the power of God in Christ.

Baptism describes the means of grace from which a slave to sin is freed and justified. Baptism sets one free from slavery to sin by Christ's death and resurrection. Baptism is a way to unite sinners with Christ, thus bestowing justification from sin and clothing them in righteousness (cf. Rom 3-5). Declared righteousness from sin comes from outside mankind, from God in Christ Jesus. Freed slaves from sin are then enslaved to Christ through Baptism (cf. Rom 6:18), having died to the reign of sin (cf. Rom 6:2, 5, 11, 18, 23). Slaves freed from sin have forgiveness of sins, and are credited righteousness on account of Christ's death and resurrection. Thereafter, freed sinners are slaves to God in Christ Jesus (cf. Rom 6:22) and transferred over from the power of sin. Sinners are handed over to the power of God under grace and life in Christ Jesus (cf. Rom 6:17-18).

Paul describes freedom and justification from slavery to sin in Romans 6. Freedom from slavery to sin equates to sinners no longer being "enslaved to sin" (Rom 6:6). Therefore, Paul describes the Baptized as "dead to sin ... [and] living to God in Christ Jesus" (Rom 6:11). As a result of Baptism, the enslaved to sin are set free and declared righteous from sin (cf. Rom 6:7, 18). The slave to God under grace is an heir of God's Kingdom as a son, on account of Christ, the Son of God. Freedom in Christ is received through faith as the gift given from God in the means of grace. Grace is issued freely for sinners.

Perhaps associating sin with slavery seems easier to accept than slavery to God and righteousness (cf. Rom

6:18-22). Although the righteousness that comes from Christ is "apart from the law"[100] (Rom 3:21; cf. Rom 10:4), it provides a kind of slavery that comes from God's grace in Baptism. Although it is nominally slavery, it is vastly different from human slavery and eternally distinct from slavery to sin. Freedom from slavery to sin begins with God, who unites a sinner to the death and resurrection of Christ. This freedom is true repentant faith given and received from "the Word of Christ" (Rom 10:17) and Baptism (cf. Rom 6:3-5) for the forgiveness of sins.[101] God's promise of unity and righteousness in and with Christ is laid out in Romans 6. Slavery to God is key to understanding Paul's usage of slavery language for the Christian Baptized into Christ.

---

[100] Paul writes, "But now, apart from the Law, a righteousness of God has been revealed and is now out in the open, while being testified to by the Law and the Prophets, that is, a righteousness of God through faith of/[in] Jesus Christ into all those who believe" (Rom 3:21-22). Righteousness of God is a righteousness from Yahweh God, "[יְהוָ֣ה וְ צִדְקֵֽנוּ] Yahweh our [צֶדֶק–tsedeq] righteousness" (Jer 23:6; 33:16; cf. Isa 25:44; Dan 9:24; Rom 3:21-22; 10:4; 1 Cor 1:30; 2 Cor 5:21; Phi 3:9), and "Yahweh is righteous" (Psalm 129:4; cf. 119:37; 145:17; Jer 12:1; Dan 9:7, 14; Rom 3:25-26). Paul explains, "For [the] righteousness of God is being revealed in it [*the Goon News*] from faith[fulness] into faith, just as it stands written: "But the righteous person will live from faith." (Rom 1:17; [*italics mine*]); "צֶדֶק" n.m. rightness, righteousness — 1. what is right, just, normal; rightness, justness, of weights and measures ... 6. *righteousness* as vindicated, *justification* in controversy with enemies and troubles, *deliverance, victory, prosperity* ... b. in name וְנִקְרָא־צֶדֶק יהוה, of Messianic king (vindicating people's cause and giving victory)." BDB, 842, cf. 841.

[101] "Repent, and each of you be baptized in the name of Jesus Christ for the forgiveness of your sins; and you will receive the gift of the Holy Spirit. 'For the promise is for you and your children and for all who are far off, as many as the Lord our God will call to Himself'" (Acts 2:38-39).

Baptism into Christ's Death and Resurrection

In Baptism, one is united with Christ's death and resurrection. Paul asks, "What then will we say? Let us persist in sin so that grace might multiply? May it never come to be! We who died to sin, how will we still live in it? Or do you not know that as many of us as were baptized into Christ Jesus, [that] we were baptized into his death?" (Rom 6:1-2). A slave to God and righteousness is free from slavery to sin, having died by Baptism into Christ's death, and is declared righteous (cf. Rom 6:7, 18, 22).

Romans 6 clearly teaches Baptismal death and resurrection in Christ Jesus. Paul writes,

> As many of us as were baptized into Christ Jesus, [that] we were baptized into his death? Consequently, we were buried with him through this Baptism into [his] death, so that just as Christ was raised from [the] dead through the glory of the Father, thus also we might walk in life's renewal. Indeed, since we have become united and grow together with the likeness of his death, we will certainly also be [united in the likeness] of his resurrection (Rom 6:3-5).

The Baptized are buried with Christ in the likeness of His death. Thereafter, Christians are raised with Christ to walk in life's renewal. Baptized believers united with Christ are freed from slavery to sin on account of Christ, therefore having died to sin's reign. The sinner, dead, buried, and raised with Christ, is "living to God in Christ" (Rom 6:11). A slave to God is alive in Christ through Baptism,

They have been freed from slavery to sin and are now enslaved to a new Master and "Lord" (κύριος). As a result, his life— eternal life—is theirs. As Jesus "died to sin once for all" and now "lives to God" (6:10), so baptized believers in him are "dead to sin" and "living to God in Christ Jesus" (6:11), who is now further defined as "our Lord" (ἐν Χριστῷ Ἰησοῦ τῷ κυρίῳ ἡμῶν, 6:23). And, once again, how did we get to be "in Christ"? "We were baptized into Christ Jesus" (6:3); therefore, he is also our Lord.[102]

The slave to the new Master, Jesus, is free from slavery to sin through faith and Baptism in Christ Jesus the Lord, "by the washing of regeneration and renewing by the Holy Spirit"[103] (Titus 3:5).

The enslaved sinner cannot be freed unless born anew by the Holy Spirit. The sinner is "by nature sinful and

[102] Middendorf, *Romans 1–8*, 509; All who are Baptized: "From that moment [Baptism into Christ] he belongs to Christ. He is wrested from the dominion of the world, and passes to the ownership of Christ. Baptism therefore betokens a breach. Christ invades the realm of Satan, and creates for himself his Church ... The baptized Christian has ceased to belong to the world and is no longer its slave. He belongs to Christ alone ..." Dietrich Bonhoeffer, *The Cost of Discipleship* (New York: Touchstone, 1995), 231; see *The Cost of Discipleship*, 227-235.

[103] Paul explains Baptism is the work of God: "But when the kindness and affection of God our Savior appeared, He saved us, not by works which we did in righteousness, but according to His mercy, through the washing of regeneration and renewing by the Holy Spirit, whom He [God] poured out upon us richly through Jesus Christ our Savior, so that having been justified by His grace, we would become heirs according to the hope of eternal life" (Titus 3:4-7; cf. John 3:5; Rom 5:5; 8:17; Eph 3:26; 1 Pet 3:21).

unclean."[104] Received by grace, the bound sinner is "(re) born"[105] anew of the Holy Spirit by Baptism into Christ and created anew as a slave to God in Christ. Sinners are the ones for whom Christ died. Paul declares, "For what he [Christ] died, he died to sin once for all" (Rom 6:10; cf. Heb 7:27; 9:12; 10:10).[106] The slave to God is sanctified, possessing true faith and holiness from God on account of Christ. Sanctification is being set apart as holy to God. Sinners are sanctified to God through Jesus Christ's sacrifice for sin. Jesus' atonement for sin was paid for by His crucified body and shed blood "once for all" (Rom 6:10; Heb 7:27; 9:12, 26; 10:10). Justification and sanctification in Christ Jesus are gracious gifts from God.

The sinner freed from slavery to sin has Christ's righteousness, justification, and sanctification through faith under grace. Pieper explains, "Strictly speaking, only that Word which mortifies the old man and supplies strength

---

[104] *Lutheran Service Book* (St, Louis, MO: Concordia Publishing House, 2006), 151, 167.

[105] Not born by human birth through the womb, but born of the Spirit as a new creature in Christ, "born again" (John 3:3, 7; 1 Pet 1:3, 23), "born of water and the Spirit" (John 3:5), born from above—born of God (cf. John 1:13; 1 John 3:9; 4:7; 5:1, 4, 18).

[106] Middendorf explains, 'Once for all' (ἐφάπαξ) is a crucial term in Hebrews (see the second textual note on 6:10). Paul's only use of the term in Romans makes essentially the same theological point as that author. Christ has completed his conquest over sin and death with finality. But there is more. The once-for-all-ness of his death to sin is the critical factor for all those who also, as Paul says, have died to sin (6:2). Our Baptism is effective because "we were baptized into his death" (6:3), which was a death "to sin once for all" (6:10)." *Romans 1–8*, 472; "ἐφάπαξ (s. ἅπαξ) adv. ① pert. to being simultaneous, *at once, at one time* ... ② taking place once and to the exclusion of any further occurrence, *once for all, once and never again* (Eupolis Com. [V B.C.] 175 Kock) Ro 6:10; Hb 7:27; 9:12; 10:10." BDAG, 417; "ἐφάπαξ ephapax; from G1909 and G530; *once for all:* — once for all." NASEC, G2178.

to the new man is the means of sanctification, namely, the Gospel (the means of grace), not the Law. It is only the Gospel which dethrones sin; the Law can only multiply sin (Rom. 6:14; 7:5-6; Jer. 31:31)."[107] Sanctification comes from the dominion of grace in the Word of Christ. Middendorf comments, "Therefore, wherever the Law causes sin to multiply, grace, like a mighty flood, overflows above and beyond our trespasses (5:20). Grace reigns!"[108] Paul writes, "Indeed, sin will not be lord of you; for you are not under Law but under grace" (Rom 6:14). Grace rules over and above the Law, covering the offense of sin. By grace, the "old man/self"[109] dies (cf. Rom 6:6; Eph 4:22; Col 3:9), and the καινὸν "ἄνθρωπον–new man/self"[110] is raised (cf. Rom 6:4; Eph. 4:24; Col 3:10). The new man in Christ is justified from sin. The new man is sanctified, freed from slavery to sin, and bound to God "in Christ"[111] through faith and Baptism into Christ. Therefore, the sinner freed from slavery to sin has Christ's righteousness, justification, and sanctification through faith under grace.

---

[107] Francis Pieper, *Christian Dogmatics*, vol. 3., 18; Scripture brings this teaching of the dominion of grace to light. Paul writes, "And the Law came in alongside that the trespass might multiply. But where sin multiplied, grace overflowed above and beyond" (Rom 5:20; cf. Rom 3:20; Gal 3:19; 1 Tim 1:14).

[108] Middendorf, *Romans 1–8*, 451–452.

[109] Cf. Chapter 2, note 91; "παλαιὸς ἡμῶν ἄνθρωπος–old [our] man/self" (Rom 6:6).

[110] "καινὸν ἄνθρωπον–new man" (Eph 4:24); "καινός, ή, όν ... ① pert. to being in existence for a relatively short time, *new, unused* ... ③ pert. to that which is recent in contrast to someth. old, *new* ... ⓑ in the sense that what is old has become obsolete, and should be replaced by what is new. . . Of the renewing of a pers. who has been converted κ. ἄνθρωπος Eph 4:24." BDAG, 496-97; "καινός kainos; a prim. word; *new, fresh:* — fresh." NASEC, G2537.

[111] Cf. Rom 5:12-21; 6:11; 1 Cor 15:21-22.

Righteousness and Justification from Sin Received

Justification is the declaration of righteousness that God imparts to sinners on account of Christ. The Baptized are freed from slavery to sin and "δεδικαιωται—*justified, declared righteous,*" [112] from sin. Paul writes, "For the one who died has been [δεδικαιωται] declared righteous and stands justified from sin" (Rom 6:7; cf. v. 11; 7:4; 8:1; Gal 2:20; Col 3:1-3; Heb 4:10; 1 Pet 3:18; 4:1). Just as the person is ruled not guilty before a judge in court, the sinner is ruled not guilty before God and stands justified from sin before God for Christ's sake. [113] Declared righteousness is called

---

[112] "δεδικαίωται—This is a perfect indicative passive of δικαιόω, and a divine passive. The meaning is, then, "he has been declared righteous [by God] and stands justified." The general reticence of English versions to translate δεδικαίωται with "righteousness/justification" terminology is odd, especially in Romans. Translations typically use "is freed" (e.g., RSV, NRSV, NASB) or "has been set free" (ESV). BDAG offers "the one who died is freed fr[om] sin" (s.v. δικαιόω, 3), though this definition of δικαιόω ("make free/pure") is given for Pauline use only here, in 1 Cor 6:11, and, possibly, 1 Tim 3:16. But translating δικαιόω with "make/ set free" loses its forensic force and is, therefore, both inadequate and theologically problematic. Paul is not saying believers are free from sin or sinning. "Make/set free" would be appropriate if the verb were ἐλευθερόω, which Paul uses later in the midst of the language of slavery (6:18, 22; cf. 6:20; 7:3)." Middendorf, *Romans 1–8*, 449; "δικαιόω ... δεδικαίωμαι Ro 6:7; 1 Cor 4:4 ... ③ to cause someone to be released from personal or institutional claims that are no longer to be considered pertinent or valid, *make free/pure* ... ἁμαρτίας *the one who died is freed fr. sin* Ro 6:7." BDAG, 249; "δικαιόω dikaioō; from G1342; *to show to be righteous, declare righteous:* — acknowledged...justice." NASEC, G1344; This book holds δεδικαίωται as "*declared righteous* and *stands justified* from sin" in Romans 6:7.

[113] Perhaps, such as in court: Once the pronounced verdict—declaration of grace and judgment is final—and as the gavel on the sounding block is called to order, no one can question or overthrow the judge's pronounced judgment and authority.

forensic justification (righteousness).[114] Justification from sin is bestowed in Baptism, in which sinners are united to Christ. God's declaration of righteousness on account of Christ is for the sinner so that the sinner "stands justified from sin" (Rom 6:7). Sinners declared righteous are born of God, saved by grace through faith (Eph 2:5–8).

As a result of faith and Baptism into Christ, slavery to sin has been abolished and overruled by God's power and righteousness. Therefore, Baptized believers are no longer under the condemnation and judgment of sin, but set free from sin, under grace, and no longer slaves to sin on account of Christ Jesus. The slave to Jesus Christ is also a slave to righteousness (cf. Rom 6:18–19).

Sinners freed from slavery to sin are now instruments of righteousness for the sake of Christ. Through faith in Christ, there is no longer condemnation (cf. John 5:24; Rom 8:1), but life in Christ "as living from [the] dead and your bodily members to God [as] instruments of righteousness" (Rom 6:13). The sinner is no longer condemned by the Law, but raised from the deadness of sin and its consequences. Thus, all freed from slavery to sin are alive from their graves in Christ alone.

---

[114] Erwin Lueker writes forensic justification is an "Act of God by which He judicially declares a sinner righteous for the sake of Christ." Lueker, *Lutheran Cyclopedia*, 304; Thomas Schreiner comments, "forensic righteousness is the basis or foundation for freedom from the power of sin. Only those who have died with Christ are declared to be righteous and thus are enabled to conquer the mastery of sin." Thomas Schreiner, *Romans*, 2nd ed., *Baker Exegetical Commentary on the New Testament* (Grand Rapids, MI: Baker Academic, 2018), 320; The conqueror of sin is declared righteous in Christ in His death and resurrection from the dead, and those in Christ are passive recipients of grace also has Christ's righteousness and victory over sin and death (cf. Rom 8:37; 1 John 5:4-5).

Righteousness from Without

Sinners have Christ's righteousness as a gift from without or outside oneself. Middendorf explains, "The righteousness of God comes to us from outside of us (*extra nos*)."[115] This righteousness is *"extra nos ipso*,[116] from outside the sinner and *"iustitia extra nos posita,"* which proclaims justification apart from the good works of the sinner.[117] Justification grants the sinner to be freed from slavery to sin, and his master is now God. As such, *extra nos* righteousness from God allows sinners to be freed from slavery to sin and instead enslaved to righteousness.

Paul furthers this point when he says, "And, after being freed from the [slavery] of sin, you were enslaved to righteousness" (Rom 6:18).[118] The reign of slavery to sin, death, and condemnation of the Law is abolished in Christ's death and resurrection, freeing sinners. Righteousness is apart from our works (cf. 3:19–20, 28; 4:4–6)—it is all a gift of God's grace through Christ (cf. Rom 5:15, 17, 18).

---

[115] Middendorf, *Romans 1–8*, 455.

[116] "extra nos ipsos = outside of ourselves." David Scaer, *A Latin Ecclesiastical Glossary: For Francis Pieper's Christian Dogmatics* (1978), 20, 29; "The righteousness of God comes to us from outside of us (*extra nos*)." Middendorf, *Romans 1–8*, 455.

[117] "iustitia extra nos posita = justification takes place apart from man's effort." Scaer, *A Latin Ecclesiastical Glossary: For Francis Pieper's Christian Dogmatics*, 20, 29.

[118] Middendorf lays out Paul's past tense speaking of slavery to sin: "But Paul states this description in the past tense: "you were slaves to sin" (6:17). What changed? The bookends of 6:17 establish the important point. The verse begins by giving "thanks ... to God" (χάρις ... τῷ θεῷ) and concludes with a divine passive, "you were handed over" (παρεδόθητε). Paul reinforces this in the very next verse, which begins with another divine passive, "after being freed" (ἐλευθερωθέντες, 6:18). Together these expressions communicate that you were delivered and freed from slavery by God and, therefore, properly give thanks to him." *Romans 1–8*, 499-500.

Eternal life is given to sinners through faith in Christ to free the captives from slavery to sin to become slaves of God, enslaved to righteousness.

Luther wrote in *Two Kinds of Righteousness*,

> The first is alien righteousness, that is the righteousness of another, instilled from without, This is the righteousness of Christ by which he justifies through faith, as written in 1 Cor 1 [:30]: 'Whom God made our wisdom, our righteousness and sanctification and redemption.' ... This righteousness, then, is given to men in baptism and whenever they are truly repentant.[119]

Luther points to Christ alone as the wisdom of God from whom sinners' righteousness comes. The Holy Spirit works repentance and faith in the sinner by bringing Christ's righteousness through Baptism. Jesus' righteousness is bestowed from outside the sinner for Christ's sake because of His payment for sinners' redemption. The slave to Christ is declared righteous, receiving what Luther describes as "alien righteousness." Through faith and Baptism, the freed slave from sin is also a new creation (cf. 2 Cor 5:17) and "created in Christ Jesus for good works" (Eph 2:10).

Freed for Life in Christ

Salvation from sin and death is the Good News. Moreover, Paul writes that the Good News is the power of God, "For I am not ashamed of the Good News, because it is [the] power

---

[119] Luther, "Two Kinds of Righteousness" (1519), *AE* 31:297.

of God into salvation for everyone who believes" (Rom 1:16; cf. 1 Cor 1:18). The Good News is Jesus Christ crucified and risen "according to the Scriptures," [120] for sinners' freedom from slavery to sin and death and for the forgiveness of sins. Thus, the Baptized are "living from the dead" (Rom 6:13), united to the death and resurrection of Christ, and free from eternal death to eternal life (cf. John 5:24; Rom 6:13).[121]

Paul clarifies unity into Christ through Baptism, "Indeed, since we have become united and grow together with the likeness of his death, we will certainly also be [united in the likeness] of his resurrection" (Rom 6:5). The Baptized have died to sin in Christ's death and died to the condemnation of the Law through Baptism into Christ. Jesus Messiah fulfilled the Law that condemned enslaved sinners "sold under sin" (cf. Rom 7:14), now free from sin and death.

As a result of sinners' death to sin and unity with Christ, on the one hand, sinners are freed from slavery to sin and, on the other hand, raised to Christ's eternal life, alive in Christ. Paul writes, "Thus you also count yourselves to be dead to sin on the one hand, but, on the other hand, living to God in Christ Jesus" (Rom 6:11). Scripture speaks of death and dying to sin when one is raised and resurrected to life with Christ.[122] Eternal life in Christ is the free gift of God, and grants freedom from the consequences of sin and death.

---

[120] Paul writes, "For I delivered to you as of first importance what I also received, that Christ died for our sins according to the Scriptures, and that He was buried, and that He was raised on the third day according to the Scriptures" (1 Cor 15:3-4; cf. Psalm 16:10; Isa 53; Matt 12:20; 16:21; Luke 24:25-27; John 1:29; 2:19-22; Acts 2:23-32; 8:32; 13:33-35; 26:22-23; Gal 1:4; Eph. 1:7; 1 Pet 2:24).

[121] "As many of us as were baptized into Christ Jesus, [that] we were baptized into his death?" (Rom 6:3).

[122] Resurrection, or being raised with Christ in Romans 6 also seen in Paul's letter to the Colossians, "Therefore, if you have been raised with Christ, keep seeking the things above, where Christ is, seated at the right hand of

In the joyful truth and reality of Christ's Kingdom, the struggle with sin remains and physical death is imminent. However, for now and forever, "the gracious gift of God is eternal life in Christ Jesus our Lord" (6:23). On the Last Day, the dead to sin will rise from physical death into everlasting life with all the saints. Even though the physical body temporarily dies, all the saints and slaves of God are looking forward to the Resurrection on the Last Day into the new heavens and new earth where death will be no more (cf. 1 Cor 15:54). Middendorf writes of the theme of "now/not yet" in Romans 6,

> Turning specifically to Romans 6, the dominant theme is the "now/not yet" relationship of believers in regard to sin. Through Baptism into Christ, believers "now" have already died to sin's slavery. Nevertheless, as long as their own physical death (as well as bodily resurrection on the Last Day) has "not yet" taken place, believers remain engaged in an ongoing struggle against sin throughout their earthly life.[123]

The slave of God struggles with sin, lives in Christ now, and has hope for the fullness of life with God forever as His joyful slaves of righteousness (cf. Rom 6:18).[124] Slavery to God and slavery to righteousness are joyous gifts of God to sinners raised to life in Christ. The sinner freed from slavery to sin is now a son and slave of God in Christ.

God ... For you died and your life has been hidden with Christ in God" (Col 3:3).

[123] Middendorf, *Romans 1–8*, 442.

[124] Cf. Isa 25:8; 60:20; 65:17-19; 66:22; Hos 13:14; Matt 24:25; Rom 6:18; 1 Cor 15: 54-58; 2 Pet 3:10; Rev 7:17; 21:1-7.

Jesus says, "The Son remains forever ... So if the Son makes you free, you will be free indeed" (John 8:35, 36).[125] Freedom from slavery to sin and death is precisely what Jesus speaks about here. Jesus Christ is the one who remains in His house forever, freeing the captives from slavery to sin. Sinners were once orphans, as "children of the devil" (1 John 3:10)—of wrath, but are now "adopted as sons" [126] of God through Christ (cf. Rom 8:15, 23; Gal 4:5). The sons of God are now slaves to God and righteousness. Saint John Chrysostom wrote of Romans 6:18,

> "Being then made free from sin, ye became the servants [slaves] of righteousness.' There are two gifts of God which he here points out. The 'freeing from sin,' and

---

[125] See the promises of God in Abraham's Offspring, the son of the promise and the son of the slave woman (cf. Gen 21:8-21; Joh 8:35; Gal 3:18; 4:21-31).

[126] Das explains adoption in Galatians: "4:5 υἱοθεσίαν ('adoption as sons')— Although daughters were sometimes adopted in the Greco-Roman world— and this may be reflected in Paul's movement from (masculine) 'sons' to (neuter, inclusive) 'children' in Rom 8:14, 16—daughters could not carry on a family line in first-century patriarchal society, and their adoptions are narrated with different terminology. Males were the only ones described by the ancients as enjoying 'adoption as sons.' Paul also prefers 'sons' (υἱοί, e.g., Gal 3:26; 4:6) over 'children' (τέκνα, in Galatians only in 4:19-31) because the adoption of baptized believers as sons is dependent upon and inextricably tied to Jesus as God's 'Son' (υἱός, 4:4; also, e.g., 1:16; 2:20), the proper heir (Norm Mundhenk, "Adoption: Being Recognized as a Son," BT 59 (2008): 169–78; Burke, *Adopted*, 21, n. 2) ... In Gal 4:4–5 Paul says that God has sent forth his Son not only to redeem those under the Law but also 'in order that we might receive the adoption as sons.' In 3:26 Paul climactically declares the Galatians to be 'sons of God in Christ,' and in 4:6 he again emphatically proclaims them God's adopted 'sons.' In the Greco-Roman world, adoption could grant even a slave the full rights and privileges of a natural son (thus 4:7). Although the Jews did not generally practice adoption in Paul's day (υἱοθεσία, Gal 4:5; cf. also Rom 9:4), the apostle is drawing on a widely recognized custom as a way of explaining the benefits of Christ's saving work." *Galatians*, Concordia Commentary, 398, 412–413.

also the 'making them servants [slaves] to righteousness,' which is better than any freedom. For God hath done the same as if a person were to take an orphan, who had been carried away by savages into their own country, and were not only to free him from captivity, but were to set a kind father over him, and bring him to very great dignity. And this has been done in our case."[127]

The orphan, free from savage captivity to sin and death, is under the care of a merciful and kind Father through the Son, Jesus.

Slaves to God in Christ Jesus

Paul identifies himself as a "[slave][128] of Christ Jesus ... set apart for the gospel" (Rom 1:1; cf. Gal 1:10; Phil 1:1; 1 Cor 9:19; Titus 1:1). Middendorf elucidates δοῦλος as a slave of Christ bought and paid for, and possession of another,

---

[127] John Chrysostom, "Homilies on Acts and Romans," vol. XI, *The Nicene and Post-Nicene Fathers,* first series, ed. by Philip Schaff, 14 vols (1886-1889, repr., Grand Rapids, MI: Eerdmans Printing Company, 1997), 412-13. Hereafter, NPNF.

[128] Middendorf notes, "1:1 Παῦλος δοῦλος Χριστοῦ Ἰησοῦ—The translation of δοῦλος as 'servant' is weak (e.g., ESV, RSV, NRSV).1 'Bondservant' is better (NKJV; similar is NASB), but 'slave' is most accurate ... The use of עֶבֶד in the OT (usually rendered as δοῦλος in the LXX) raises the status of certain people who are referred to as Yahweh's 'servant' (e.g., Moses in Josh 1:2; Samuel in 1 Sam 3:9–10; David in 2 Sam 3:18; 7:5, 8). However, even in relationship to God or, as here, to Christ Jesus, the point remains that the δοῦλος is 'owned body and soul' (BDAG, 2 b β) by him." *Romans 1–8,* 57.

Immediately after his name, he describes himself as a δοῦλος. Being "a slave of Christ Jesus" means he is bought, paid for, and owned by Christ (as in Phil 1:1; see also Titus 1:1; cf. James 1:1; 2 Pet 1:1; Jude 1). The secular use of the word readily conveys the notion of being owned by another (see the textual note). Paul affirms the idea for the Corinthians by reminding them: "and you are not your own, for you were purchased at a price" (1 Cor 6:19–20). Being a δοῦλος, "slave," expresses Jesus' ownership of Paul (and us), but it also points ahead toward the type of κύριος, "Lord," Jesus is, namely, one who faithfully sacrificed himself for us and who seeks to conform our will to his own (see, e.g., 3:21–26; 12:1–2; see also Mt 20:25–28; Jn 13:13–17).[129]

The slave of Christ is bought and owned, ransomed and redeemed by Christ through faith and Baptism. For as Paul writes, "You were bought with a price" (1 Cor 6:20; 7:23).[130]

Slaves of God are slaves of Jesus Christ. Paul further explains, "For he who was called in the Lord while a slave, is the Lord's freedman. Likewise, he who was called while free, is Christ's slave. You were bought with a price; do not become slaves of men" (1 Cor 7:22-23; cf. 1 Cor 6:20; 1 Pet 1:18-19). Interestingly, the imperative to "not become slaves

---

129 Middendorf, *Romans 1–8*, 61-62; "'Everybody's Serving Someone,' is validated by Romans 6." Ibid.

130 For "ransom" and "redeemed" references, cf., Matt 20:28; Mark 10:45; Luke 1:68; Acts 7:35; 20:28; Gal 3:13; 4:5; 1 Tim 2:6; Titus 2:14; 1 Pet 1:18; Rev 5:9; 14:3-4.

of men" (1 Cor 7:23) would be to deny the freedom from sin and Satan through Christ's payment for sin and respond again to sin and death.[131] Furthermore, being called by God to freedom through faith is indeed why "Paul begins by referring to himself as 'a slave of Christ Jesus'."[132] Fittingly, the slave to Christ is a slave to righteousness.

Paul is not alone in describing himself as a slave to Christ. In Philippians chapter one, Paul describes himself and Timothy as "slaves of Christ Jesus" (v. 1). Paul and Silas are called slaves of God (cf. Acts 16:17. In fact, all the Baptized believers are "freed from the [slavery] of sin . . . enslaved to God" (Rom 6:22). Therefore, note these examples:

- Epaphras "a slave of Christ Jesus" (Col 4:12),
- God's workmen are "the Lord's slaves" (2 Tim 2:24),
- "James, a slave of God and of the Lord Jesus Christ" (James 1:1), and
- "Free people ... as slaves of God" (cf. 1 Pet 2:16),
- "Simeon Peter, a slave and apostle of Jesus Christ" (2 Pet 1:1), and
- "Jude, a slave to Jesus Christ" (Jude 1:1).
- Jesus' mother identifies as a slave of Yahweh, "And Mary said, Behold, the slave of the Lord; may it be

---

[131] Paul E. Kretzmann commented, "The price of redemption which had to be laid down to deliver us from the slavery of sin and Satan was so immeasurably great that it must serve for all times to deter us from a very -foolish step, that of becoming servants of men, of selling ourselves into the vilest of slavery by abandoning the truth of Scriptures and permitting ourselves to be swayed and governed by the imagination and wisdom of men. And the Corinthians could readily make the application of the word in their own case, namely, not to make themselves so dependent upon any man as to imagine that they were not really free, even though they had a master over them." Paul E. Kretzmann, *Popular Commentary of the Bible: The New Testament*, 2 vols, 121.

[132] Middendorf, *Romans 1–8*, 503.

done to me according to your word … And my spirit has rejoiced in God my Savior. 'For He has looked upon the humble state of His slave" (Luke 1:38, 47-48).

- Simeon in the temple, "Now Master, You are releasing Your slave in peace, According to Your word" (Luke 2:29). Along with all the saints, God's people are slaves of Christ.

- John speaks the same way in the Book of Revelation in the first chapter: "his slave John" (Rev 1:1) and the 144,000 sealed "slaves of our God" (Rev 7:3), and "his own slaves, the prophets" (Rev 10:7) and Yahweh's "slaves, the prophets, and to the saints and to those who fear your name, the small and the great" (Rev 11:18). Moses, the slave of God (Rev 15:3), the blood of God's slaves shed by the great harlot (cf. Rev 19:2), and "all you slaves, and those who fear him, the small and the great" (Rev. 19:5), the angel and fellow slave with the brothers (cf. Rev 19:10; 22:9), the Lamb's slaves (cf. Rev 22:3), and Yahweh's slaves (cf. Rev 22:6).

The Old Testament LXX, read by Jesus and Paul in the first century, also beautifully identifies the language of the slave of God. The Septuagint is undoubtedly familiar with δοῦλοι τοῦ θεοῦ––the slaves of God. Consider these examples: Ezra and all rebuilding the temple, as "slaves of God" (cf. Ezra 5:11; Isa 42:19). Joshua and Moses identify themselves individually as a δοῦλος κυρίου––slave of Yahweh (cf. Josh 14:7; Judges 2:8; 2 Kings 18:12).[133]

---

[133] The Septuagint, "Greek Old Testament" rendered in these verses are δοῦλοι τοῦ θεοῦ–slaves of God, and δοῦλος κυρίου–slaves of Yahweh. In contrast, English translations render the Old Testament; "servant(s)

Spiritual slavery to God in Christ embodies a Spirit of gentleness, as well as gratitude and thankfulness in response to being bought from sin through Yahweh's promised Messiah, Jesus. The slave of Christ is revealed clearly in the Scripture as redeemed by God to live in Christ's Kingdom.

Transfer of Power and Status "Handed Over"

Enslaved sinners are transferred, or handed over, from the power and kingdom of Satan over to the power and Kingdom of Christ (cf. Col 1:13). The slave to sin is now a slave to God, declared righteous by God in Christ. Slaves to sin become transferred over as slaves to God by the acquittal of sin and declaration of righteousness on account of Christ.

Slavery to God is a transfer of authority from Satan's power. In the Book of Acts, Paul describes the transfer of authority from darkness to light, from the power of Satan to God, before King Agrippa.[134] Paul writes of this status change, "But thanks [be] to God, because you were slaves of sin, but you responded from [the] heart to [the] form of teaching into which you were handed over. Furthermore,

---

of Yahweh (the LORD)" and "servant(s) of the Most High God" instead of "slaves of …" in these verses and others. Cf. Hebrew עַבְדִּי־הֳוָהַ–slave of Yahweh, and הֳלָא־יִד יהודבע–slaves of the Most High God (cf. Dan 3:33, 43/44, 46, 86, 93).

[134] "And I said, 'Who are you, Lord?' And the Lord said, 'I am Jesus whom you are persecuting. But rise up and stand on your feet; for this purpose I have appeared to you, to appoint you as a servant [υπηρετην] and a witness not only to the things in which you have seen, but also to the those in which I will appear to you; rescuing you from the Jewish people and from the Gentiles, to whom I am sending you; to open their eyes so that they may turn from darkness to light and from the authority [ἐξουσία] of Satan to God, that they may receive forgiveness of sins and an inheritance among those who have been sanctified by faith in me'" (Acts 26:15-18 cf. Col 1:13-4).

after being freed from the [slavery] of sin, you were enslaved to righteousness" (Rom 6:17-18). Slaves of sin are handed over as slaves to Christ. Slavery language used by Paul helps the reader and recipient of grace to see the handing over of lordship as exclusively the work of God and not due to the individual's works, will, choice, merits, or righteousness.

Being handed over to Master Jesus Christ is the work and will of God in Christ through the Word and Baptism, where faith is created and given by the Holy Spirit. Middendorf comments on being handed over to another master,

> The metaphor of slavery developed by Paul in 6:16–22 supports understanding the verb "handed over" as connoting slaves (of sin) being "handed over" to another master, namely, the Lord Jesus. The concept of the transfer of a slave also indicates that the verb functions as a divine passive. The notion that "you were handed over [by God]" (παρεδόθητε) makes clear that this change in status is not effected by a person's works or his decision; neither is it a matter of active obedience. As with the numerous passives regarding Baptism earlier in the chapter (e.g., 6:3, 4, 6, 7), Paul's language here is precise.[135]

Handed over as a slave to God as a result of Baptism, the sinner is under the power of Christ.

Those enslaved to righteousness are born of God and no longer of the world or under the power of Satan. John

---

[135] Middendorf, *Romans 1–8*, 501.

writes, "We know that no one who has been born of God sins, but He who was begotten of God keeps him, and the evil one does not touch him. We know that we are of God, and the whole world lies in the power of the evil one" (1 John 5:18-19; cf. John 8:23; 15:19; 17:14, 16; 18:36). Slaves of God are handed over from the darkness into light, from the evil one and slavery to sin, to slavery to God. Paul explains it is Jesus Christ, "who rescued us from the authority of darkness, and transferred us to the kingdom of the Son of His love, in whom we have redemption, the forgiveness of sins" (Col 1:13-14; cf. Acts 26:18). Transferred over from the authority of Satan to God through repentant faith and Baptism into Christ, God forgives sinners of all sin—past, present, and future.

Conclusion

Thankfully, Christians have been handed over as slaves to Christ who redeemed those who were once captive to the world and the power of sin, death, and evil.[136] Slavery to sin has ended for the Baptized believer; the old self has been "crucified with Christ" (Gal 2:20). The body of sin has been brought to nothing. The sinner is no longer enslaved to sin (cf. Rom 6:6) but set free, declared righteous, and justified from sin (cf. Rom 6:7, 18). Therefore, those bound to God in Christ Jesus rejoice as slaves to God and righteousness, receiving a righteousness *extra nos*—from without or outside themselves. The slave of God is also resurrected from the

---

[136] The psalmist sings of the redemption of God from the power of Sheol. "But God will redeem my soul from the power of Sheol, for He will receive me" (Psalm 49:15; cf. Psalm 16:10; Hos 13:14; Acts 2:27; 1 Cor 15:16; Heb 2:14.

spiritual deadness of sin to eternal life in Christ. The sinner has been handed over from the power of Satan to God in Christ. Paul concludes Romans 6, "For the payment of sin is death, but the gracious gift of God is eternal life in Christ Jesus our Lord" (Rom 6:23),[137] giving an exemplary description of the work of God in Christ for sinners.

The slave to God looks forward to Jesus' Parousia and the resurrection on the Last Day. Baptized believers will be fully transformed into the new heaven and new earth. Middendorf writes, "While our full experience of life with Christ remains in the future (our bodily resurrection will take place when Christ returns on the Last Day), already now the promise is certain for 'as many as of us as were baptized into Christ Jesus' (6:3)."[138]

In the next chapter, the slave to God and righteousness presents bodily members to Christ and bears fruit in sanctification. Martin Luther wrote, "To make the way

---

[137] Middendorf elucidates: "Thankfully, the last half of 6:23 provides the rest of the story.84 Paul expresses the positive, antithetical alternative as "the gracious gift of God." Thus God's "gracious gift" (χάρισμα), previously used in 5:15 and 5:16, is now equated with "eternal life" (ζωὴ αἰώνιος), mentioned earlier in 2:7; 5:21; 6:22. This makes clear how the outcome just stated with the same words at the end of 6:22 is attained. Such life is not obtained by producing fruit or through consecrated living, significant as those are. It is, instead, the gracious gift of God "in Christ Jesus our Lord" (6:23). The lordship of sin and its reign have been deposed by Jesus Christ and now stand opposed by those in him ("continually resist the reign of sin," 6:12; "sin will not be lord of you," 6:14). They have been freed from slavery to sin and are now enslaved to a new Master and "Lord" (κύριος). As a result, his life—eternal life—is theirs. As Jesus "died to sin once for all" and now "lives to God" (6:10), so baptized believers in him are "dead to sin" and "living to God in Christ Jesus" (6:11), who is now further defined as "our Lord" (ἐν Χριστῷ Ἰησοῦ τῷ κυρίῳ ἡμῶν, 6:23). And, once again, how did we get to be "in Christ"? "We were baptized into Christ Jesus" (6:3); therefore, he is also our Lord." *Romans 1–8*, 509.

[138] Ibid., 470.

smoother for the unlearned—for only them do I serve—I shall set down the following two propositions concerning the freedom and the bondage of the spirit: A Christian is perfectly free lord of all, subject to none. A Christian is a dutiful servant of all, subject to all."[139] Those bound to Christ and His righteousness are subject to none and, yet, also willingly subject to all. Similarly, Paul expresses a positive kind of slavery in the second half of Romans 6. The next chapter explores what slavery to righteousness looks like within Paul's imperatives to Christian slaves of righteousness.

---

[139] Luther, "Freedom of a Christian" (1520), *AE* 31:344.

St. Paul (First State) (1514), by Albrecht Dürer

Four

Redeemed Slaves to Righteousness and to God

In Romans 6, Paul exhorts those who have received grace, sanctification, and a new life in Christ to enslave themselves to God and to righteousness itself. This chapter explores what sanctified living in Christ "looks like." Slaves of Christ are imperatively exhorted to sanctified living through Christ, which is enabled by the indicative grace given through salvation. In other words, imperative exhortations for sanctified Christian living are only possible by the indicative Word of grace in the Good News that freely justifies sinners on account of Christ. Saints of God are slaves of righteousness—slaves of Christ, the "Righteous One" (Isa 53:11; Acts 7:52; 22:14). Therefore, the saints of God serve as slaves to righteousness. Paul most clearly uses slavery language in the latter half of Romans 6:12-23.

Slaves of righteousness live on account of Christ in His Kingdom in repentant faith through the means of grace. Those Baptized into Christ respond to exhortations to live holy lives in righteousness and sanctification. Paul exhorts saints of God with imperatives to righteous living as saints of God, living a new life set apart and enslaved to God and to righteousness. Saints of God are also, at the same time, righteous (just) and sinners—*simul iustus et peccator.* Therefore, they are exhorted to resist "the reign of sin" (Rom 6:12) and evil, and to present themselves to God as slaves of righteousness (cf. Rom 6:18, 19). Redeemed slaves of God under grace present their bodily members as instruments of righteousness, responding appropriately to God's imperatives as slaves of righteousness "leading to sanctification" (Rom 6:19). Slavery to righteousness in Christ is living sanctified lives under grace in Christ's Kingdom.

One's initial reaction to the suggestion that being bound to God in Christ leads to good slavery is probably, "Really? Why and how?" Being bound to God is a form of good slavery which leads to salvation through faith in the Good News. Good slavery comes from God's gift of life everlasting through faith in Jesus Christ, crucified and risen. Sinners are released from eternal captivity to sin. Slavery to sin is bad slavery. After being freed from slavery to sin, they live under grace as slaves to God and righteousness, "having fruit for sanctification" (Rom 6:22). The slave to God is fruitful in good works produced from faith in Christ.[140] The sanctified fruit produced by the slaves of Christ is from God, is good, "and the outcome is life eternal" (Rom 6:22).

Essentially, good slavery is being enslaved to righteousness and living to God in Christ. Therefore, good slavery is living out Christ's righteousness. Redeemed slaves to righteousness and God respond thankfully to the indicative grace promised in the Good News of Jesus.

---

[140] Good slavery is grace, and life that produces only good fruit (good works) is directly opposed to bad slavery of sin and death that produces only bad fruit, which only comes from spiritual slavery to sin; For bad fruit and bad slavery, cf. Chapter 2.

Baptism and Sanctification

The promised Messiah frees and justifies unrighteous sinners from sin through Baptism and into sanctified Christian living as slaves of God, responsive to righteous exhortations. A look at Baptism and sanctification should help explain how the Christian lives under grace as a slave to God and righteousness.

The slave of God is sanctified and joyful in faith possessing life everlasting by grace. Grothe comments, "God is sanctifying. And so the Christian person, under grace, kept in faith, is freed– to serve (6:18) and to rejoice (5:11). Such is the happy life of the one who lets himself be made a slave of the God who justifies the ungodly and graciously gives the gift of eternal life (6:23)."[141] Eternal life is the declarative grace of Christ's life given for sinners' justification. God's gracious gift is bestowed in Baptism.

Paul speaks explicitly of life's renewal (cf. Rom 6:4) in Christ already now. The one who is "dead to sin and alive to God in Christ Jesus" (Rom 6:11) becomes a slave to God and righteousness as a result of being buried with Christ through Baptism and raised with Him to new life (cf. Rom 6:3, 4). Pieper writes,

> Also, sanctification, the death of the old man and the resurrection to a new life, is not only typified by Baptism, but actually effected. In Rom. 6:1-11 Paul teaches that the Christians are dead unto sin, but alive unto God. This, however, is an effect of Baptism (διὰ τοῦ βαπτίσματος). Sanctification according to both its negative (dead unto sin) and its positive side (alive

---

[141] Jonathan F. Grothe, *The Justification of the Ungodly: An Interpretation of Romans*, 2nd ed. (St. Catharines, Ontario, Canada: 2012), 299.

unto God in Christ Jesus) is a *status quo* created through Baptism.[142]

This sanctification received from the indicative grace in Baptism results in the ability to "walk in life's renewal" (Rom 6:4).[143]

These indicatives are followed by imperative instructions for Christians. Christian living is explicitly for slaves of righteousness. The slave of righteousness is the slave of Christ. In other words, without indicative grace, faith and Baptism into Christ, all imperatives lead to worthless and fruitless evil deeds. But, united with Christ, slaves of righteousness are enabled to resist sin because they are under the dominion of grace and no longer under the Law (6:14).

Indicative and Imperative

Romans 6 consists of "indicative"[144] declarations of grace followed by "imperative"[145] exhortations for

---

142 Francis Pieper, *Christian Dogmatics*, vol. 3 (St. Louis, MO: Concordia Publishing House, 1953), 270.

143 "[Jesus] resurrection enables the opportunity of walking "in life's renewal" (6:4). The indicative realities which exist because of Baptism, as expressed in 6:1–11, are being applied to daily life." Middendorf, *Romans 1–8*, 495.

144 Indicative — "The mood in which the action of the verb or the state of being it describes is presented by the writer as real. It is the mood of assertion, where the writer portrays something as actual (as opposed to possible or contingent on intention). Depending on context, the writer may or may not believe the action is real, but is presenting it as real." Michael S. Heiser and Vincent M. Setterholm, *Glossary of Morpho-Syntactic Database Terminology* (Lexham Press, 2013); Douglas Mangum observes, "indicative mood — The verbal mood used for simple declarative statements." *The Lexham Glossary of Theology* (Bellingham, WA: Lexham Press, 2014).

145 Imperative — "The mood that normally expresses a command, intention, exhortation, or polite request. The imperative mood is therefore not an

Christian living.[146] Indicative statements of grace chiefly begin Romans 6, followed by further indicatives along with imperatives in order to instruct Christ's Church to live as slaves of righteousness bearing good fruit. Middendorf states,

> The key theological point is that the predominant indicative statements continue to form the basis upon which imperatives are issued and properly received. Jesus Christ has delivered us from sin and death (indicative statements of grace). His salvation, which we receive through Baptism and faith, empowers us to respond to his exhortations (imperatives) to live as freed children of God.[147]

---

expression of reality but possibility and volition." Heiser, *Glossary of Morpho-Syntactic Database Terminology*; Erwin Lueker interestingly distinguishes the categorical imperative and the hypothetical, "Categorical Imperative. Universal and unconditional moral command or obligation; distinguished from hypothetical imperative, which is conditional and depends e.g., on expediency, practical necessity, or desire." Erwin Lueker, *Lutheran Cyclopedia*, (St. Louis, MO: Concordia Publishing House, 1975), 143.

[146] "The eighteen indicative statements which permeate 6:12–23 counter the tendency to view it predominantly as imperative commands, only four of which occur. But it would also obscure Paul's purpose to exclude the exhortations to continually resist sin and, instead, to present one's entire self to God in righteousness, which has fruit for sanctified living. To highlight either the indicatives alone or the imperatives alone is a false alternative. The key, of course, is to consider both fully, with proper balance, and in the right order. The indicatives of God come first in 6:1–11, and they also lead throughout 6:12–23. The free gifts of God are passively received through Baptism and in faith. But Paul also calls for, indeed, even commands, a response which entails active resistance against sin, as well as the offering of one's bodily members in righteous service and for fruitful holy living to God." Middendorf, *Romans 1–8*, 509–510.

[147] Ibid., 484.

By the indicative, the sinner is a freed child of God who has been declared righteous from slavery to sin (cf. Rom 6:3-5). Thus, empowered to live in Christ's righteousness, these imperatives instruct sanctified Christians to live as slaves of righteousness. Middendorf writes of the indicative and imperatives in Romans 6, saying, "In 6:1–11, we are, for the most part, depicted as passive recipients of God's bounty through Baptism into Christ. Similarly, in 6:12–23, the dominant actor is God. At the same time, active verbs and imperatives punctuate this latter half of Romans 6."[148] In other words, the slave to God is passive in receiving Christ in the indicative, and then exhorted to imperatives as an appropriate and active response as slaves.

Slavery to God and righteousness means living in Christ's righteousness and His Kingdom. Christ's Kingdom reigns "now," which is here and now, on earth and in heaven, and "not yet" to come in the new heavens and new earth. The Kingdom of Christ here and now will be fully consummated on the resurrection on the Last Day. Middendorf explains now/not yet in terms of righteousness and sin:

> For those who received the righteousness of God through faith in Christ, Paul expresses the present reality 'now' with indicative forms. The ongoing negative impacts of sin, the Law, and death, which have 'not yet' been resolved by the believers' resurrection, lead to the need for his imperative exhortations.[149]

---

[148] Ibid., 510; Notably, "Romans 1-11 has 13 imperatives. But aside from the 5 in 6:11-19, Roman 1-10 has only 1, with God as the subject (3:4)! Romans 12-16 has 49 imperatives." Cf. Middendorf, *Romans 9-16*, 1193-1202.

[149] Middendorf, *Romans 1-8*, 441.

Here and now, in the present, sin remains a threat to be extinguished forever on the Last Day. Now/not yet enforces the idea that Christians are slaves of Christ who need to be exhorted to live sanctified lives now and until the Last Day.

Slavery to righteousness is slavery given by the grace of God through faith and Baptism. In other words, this good slavery is passively received on account of Christ's actions through faith alone for Christ's sake. Then, slaves of Christ are exhorted to respond appropriately in doing good.

Resisting the Reign of Sin

Here and now, slaves to God and righteousness struggle to resist sin and temptations to sin. Dedicated sanctified living remains a struggle (cf. Rom 6:11-19). Middendorf observes, "In 6:11-19, Paul uses five imperatives to exhort the Baptized to resist sin, and instead, to offer themselves in willing service to God."[150] To resist sin and offer oneself willingly exemplifies the responsiveness of a slave to God and to righteousness. The struggle persists in this present age (cf. Rom 7:7-25). Paul urges, "Therefore continually resist the reign of sin in your mortal body which results in being responsive to its desires" (Rom 6:12). Responding to the desires of the sinful flesh is not resisting sin. The implication that sin is a struggle gives the reason for this imperative to resist sin's attempts to regain its reign in the mortal flesh.

Additionally, Paul addresses resisting sin already at the beginning of Romans 6: "What then will we say? Let us persist in sin so that grace might multiply? May it never come to be! We who died to sin, how will we still live in it?" (6:1-2). Paul's rhetoric implies an existing struggle against sin in

---

[150] Middendorf, *Romans 9-16*, 1196.

the mortal body (cf. Rom 6:12), and to offer oneself willingly to serve God in righteousness for the sake of Christ. The slave of Christ should not persist in sin to multiply sin, but persist in righteousness that multiplies on account of Christ's grace.

The imperatives to resist sin and the desires of the flesh are vital to counterattacking the stench of sin. Sin is an offensive failure that falls short of God's glory. The term "sin" is derives from "ἁμαρτία-hamartia, *a sin, failure*."[151] Yet grace covers the sinners' offenses on account of Christ. By grace the Christian is also freed from sin's bondage, and then exhorted to sanctified living, which involves resisting sin.

In the now/not yet, sin remains a struggle in mortal human hearts. The renewed slave to God battles with the human nature and desire to sin. The imperatives of Paul are only applicable to those in Christ who remain *simul iustus et peccator*. Middendorf warns against misunderstandings of the *simul iustus et peccator*:[152]

> Paul's exhortations make no sense to an unbeliever; they make no sense to those who are still slaves to sin, even if that slavery

---

[151] "ἁμαρτία, ίας, ἡ ... ① a departure fr. either human or divine standards of uprightness ② *sin* ... ③ a destructive evil power, *sin* ... Sin under Law: NTS 14, '67/68, 424–39), reigns there vs. 21; 6:14; everything was subject to it Gal 3:22; people serve it Ro 6:6; are its slaves vss. 17, 20; are sold into its service 7:14 or set free from it 6:22; it has its law 7:23; 8:2; it revives (ἀνέζησεν) Ro 7:9 or is dead vs. 8; it pays its wages, viz., death 6:23, cp. 5:12 (see lit. s.v. ἐπί 6c). As a pers. principle it dwells in humans Ro 7:17, 20, viz., in the flesh (s. σάρξ 2cα) 8:3; cp. vs. 2; 7:25. The earthly body is hence a σῶμα τῆς ἁ. 6:6 (Col 2:11 v.l.).—As abstr. for concr. τὸν μὴ γνόντα ἁ. ὑπὲρ ἡμῶν ἁμαρτίαν ἐποίησεν (God) *made him, who never sinned, to be sin* (i.e. the guilty one) *for our sakes* 2 Cor 5:21." BDAG, 50-51; "ἁμαρτία hamartia; from G264; *a sin, failure:* — sin." NASEC, G266.

[152] Compare *simul iustus et peccator* with *pecca fortiter*–"sin boldly"; e.g., Luther said: "Be a sinner and sin boldly, but believe and rejoice in Christ even more boldly, for he is victorious over sin, death, and the world." *AE* 48:282; Cf. Bonhoeffer, *The Cost of Discipleship*, 52-53.

is cleverly masquerading itself as slavery to some supposedly autonomous self. The ongoing struggle expressed in 6:12–23 also betrays the notion that holiness of living is somehow temporally attainable, rather than a continual battle this side of eternity. Yet they also do not make sense if our struggle against sin and our efforts to live for God are a matter of complete futility and, therefore, not to be energetically pursued. Such resignation to sin is an improper appropriation of Luther's "sin boldly" and a simplistic misapplication of *simul justus et peccator*. Both Paul's indicatives *and* his imperatives are also not properly comprehended if one adopts a "God-does-it-all-so-I-can-be-lazy" attitude toward sanctified living. Yes, God does it all in our justification (e.g., 3:21–26, 28). We do well to reject all moralism and legalism. At the same time, we ought to confess that an indolent apathy is not what Paul teaches about sanctification.[153]

Imperative statements to the unbeliever are incomprehensible and hidden to those who struggle against sin apathetically and are under moralistic legalism. Slaves to Christ are justified from sin and sanctified, set apart as holy to God on account of Christ. That is why they struggle with the sinful nature.

---

[153] Middendorf, *Romans 1–8*, 510; "As the Formula of Concord states: 'From this it follows that as soon as the Holy Spirit has initiated his work of regeneration and renewal in us through the Word and the holy sacraments, it is certain that we can and must cooperate by the power of the Holy Spirit, even though we still do so in great weakness.' (FC SD II 65)." Ibid., 511.

Peter similarly speaks of the freedom from sin, exhorting sanctified Christians to live in Christ in responsiveness to righteousness and not for responsiveness to evil and sin. He writes, "Live as free people, but do not use your freedom as a cover-up for evil; live as God's slaves" (1 Pet 2:16). Luther also observed the Christian struggle with sin:

> The Christian life is, namely, a trial, warfare, and struggle. It is clear how those who are being tried by various shocks are to be trained, so that they do not despair if they have not yet felt that they are free from the evil prompting of any sin whatever. Thus in Rom. 13:14 Paul says: "And make no provision for the flesh, to gratify its desires." And in Rom. 6:12 he says: "Let not sin reign in your mortal bodies, to make you obey its passions." No one can avoid desire, but it is possible for us to keep from obeying the desires.[154]

In short, the Christian demonstrates these truths of sanctified living under grace as an instrument of righteousness fighting to resist the reign of sin and evil in the body.

Instruments of Righteousness

On the positive side, the Christian is to be an instrument [ὅπλα][155] of righteousness under grace. After being freed

---

[154] Luther, "Lectures on Galatians Chapters 1-6" (1519), *AE* 27:361.

[155] "ὅπλα ἀδικίας—The neuter noun ὅπλον denotes an 'instrument' or 'tool' (BDAG, 1). It can have the military connotation of a 'weapon' (BDAG, 2, citing 2 Cor 6:7; 10:4), but the more general sense applies here. The plural form ὅπλα here, along with μέλη, forms a double accusative construction,

and declared righteous from sin, Paul exhorts Christians to live in sanctification, presenting themselves as instruments of righteousness. Paul writes: "And do not continue to present your bodily members to sin [as] instruments of unrighteousness; instead, present yourselves to God as living from [the] dead and your bodily members to God [as] instruments of righteousness" [156] (Rom 6:13; cf. 2 Cor 6:7). Paul's second imperative here is to offer one's body as an instrument of God living from the dead in Christ. This recalls the previous exhortation to resist the reign of sin in the body (cf. Rom 6:12). An instrument of righteousness lives to righteousness as a slave to God. One could say that a Christian is a tool and weapon of God for righteous living.

Not Under Law but Under Grace

The slave to Christ is no longer under "Law"[157] but under "grace"[158] (cf. Rom 6:14-15). One may think that the

---

necessitating the insertion of 'as' in translation. ὅπλα is then modified by the genitive of ἀδικία, 'unrighteousness' (see the third textual note on 1:18; also 1:29; 2:8; 3:5; 9:14), but later in the verse it is used with the dative of δικαιοσύνη, 'righteousness.'" Middendorf, *Romans 1–8*, 488.

[156] Notably, the words of Paul are echoed in *The Letter of Polycarp to the Philippians* as an imperative for the church to be armed with weapons of righteousness and follow the commandment to love God and love neighbor and not the world and money. Polycarp wrote, "But the love of money is the beginning of all troubles. Knowing, therefore, that we brought nothing into the world and cannot take anything out, let us arm ourselves with the weapons of righteousness, and let us first teach ourselves to follow the commandment of the Lord" (4:1). Michael W. Holmes, *The Apostolic Fathers: Greek Texts and English Translations*, 3rd ed. (Grand Rapids, MI: Baker Academic, 2007), 285.

[157] Law—"νόμος-nomos, *that which is assigned, hence usage, law:* — Law." NASEC, G355; See BDAG, 677- 78; Cf. note 90.

[158] Grace—"χάρις-charis, *a prim. word; grace, kindness:* — blessing," NASEC, G5485; "χάριν . . . ③ practical application of goodwill, (a sign of)

Law is bad, which would be completely wrong.[159] Sin is bad, not the Law/Torah—*Decalogue*. Being under grace serves as the foundation for everything. Paul writes, "Indeed, sin will not be lord of you; for you are not under Law but under grace" (Rom 6:14). To be clear, being "under Law"[160] means to be under the entirety and perfection of the Law's demands. Falling short of the requirements of the Law is sin. Being under Law and falling short results in slavery to sin and death. God's good and perfect Law exposes and brings knowledge of sin (cf. Rom 3:20; 7:7, 13-14; Gal 3:22). Paul Kretzmann commented on Paul's statement of the being under grace and not the Law:

> For sin will not rule over you, it will not gain the ascendancy again. And the reason is: For not are you under the Law, but under grace. The Law ever demands, but does not give the strength to perform its demands, and therefore it cannot deliver from the dominion of sin. But grace, under which we have placed ourselves in conversion,

---

favor, gracious deed/gift, benefaction … ⓑ on the part of God and Christ; the context will show whether the emphasis is upon the possession of divine favor as a source of blessings for the believer, or upon a store of favor that is dispensed, or a favored status (i.e. standing in God's favor) that is brought about, or a gracious deed wrought by God in Christ, or a gracious work that grows fr. more to more (so in contrast to the old covenant Mel., P. 3, 16 al.) … Christians stand ὑπὸ χάριν under God's gracious will as expressed in their release from legal constraint Ro 6:14f, or they come ὑπὸ τὸν ζυγὸν τῆς χάριτος αὐτοῦ 1 Cl 16:17 (ζυγός 1)." BDAG, 1079, 1080.

[159] Cf. Todd Wilkon, "Is the Law Bad," *Issues Etc.* (2016): 5-17, accessed 05/09/2022, https://podcast.issuesetc.org/winter2016.pdf.

[160] Under Law—"ὑπὸ νόμον." Being under Law is not Gospel and being under grace, for the sinner is under Law condemned by the Law because of transgressions since the payment of sin and death, and the Law exposes sin.

in Baptism, not only delivers us from the guilt and power of sin, but also gives us the ability to withstand sin, to shun the evil, and to do that which pleases the Lord. Thus we renounce all dependence upon our own merit and strength, accept the offer of grace, of free justification as a gift of God, and receive deliverance from sin and the power to please our heavenly Father.[161]

The Law holds captive the sinner under the condemnation of sin. The sinner under Law is not justified by the Law, and cannot live by the Law. In contrast, the slave to Christ under grace is not under the Law or justified by the Law, but through faith and Baptism into Jesus Christ. The slave to God lives under grace in Christ's righteousness (cf. Gal 2:21; 5:24).

Baptized believers live *under grace* as responsive slaves of God, freed and declared righteous from sin. In response to Christ's grace in the Good News, believers live as slaves to God and slaves to all. Grace is the power of God empowering slaves of Christ to serve Him and His creatures. A slave to God and righteousness is a good slavery in Christ.

Therefore, being "under grace"[162] means the slave to sin and death is now "living from the dead" (Rom 6:13), justified from sin, and living to God in Christ Jesus. Therefore, the slave to Christ should not present bodily members to the unrighteousness that once ruled as lord. The slave of Christ should live in responsiveness to grace for righteousness, leading to sanctification (cf. Rom 6:19).

---

[161] Kretzmann, *Popular Commentary of the Bible*, 32.

[162] Under grace—"ὑπὸ χάριν;" Being under grace in Christ is the Gospel through faith and Baptism and a slave to God in Christ and slave to righteousness in the Gospel of Christ.

Slavery language used by Paul is an analogous teaching according to the "weakness of your flesh" (Rom 6:19). Middendorf comments on Paul's "speaking in human terms" in Romans 6:19:

> At long last, a number of apparent contradictions, at least from a human viewpoint, need to be addressed. How is one both freed and enslaved at the same time? How can there possibly be a willing enslavement which is passively received? And how can all this possibly take place "under grace" (6:14–15)? Perhaps with some exasperation, Paul declares, "I am speaking in human terms on account of the weakness of your flesh" (6:19). On the one hand, Paul loves to use numerous earthly analogies to convey the fullness of the Good News of God in Jesus Christ. On the other hand, all metaphors fall short in some way. In this case, his use of slavery is at least potentially misunderstood and, perhaps, even scandalous to his hearers.[163]

People in Paul's day would have comprehended the language of slavery. Slavery language is a human way of relating to God's theological truth and remains divinely inspired, God's language revealed for His people.

The saints of God serve Jesus Christ under grace in sanctification. Sanctification does not come from observing the Law, but through faith in the promised Messiah.

---

[163] Middendorf, *Romans 1–8*, 502–503.

Sanctification comes from God in Christ through the Holy Spirit (Titus 3:4–8). Christians are exhorted to be devoted to good works as saints/slaves bound to God in Christ. Pieper wrote of the Law in sanctification serving the Gospel:

> The Law has its place in sanctification, it serves the Gospel ... The Church is holy (*sancta ecclesia*, communion of saints), (a) because by faith in Christ all members possess the perfect righteousness of faith (*iustitia fidei imputata*,). Phil. 3:9: "Not having mine own righteousness, which is of the Law, but that which is through the faith of Christ, the righteousness which is of God by faith"; (b) because all members have also a true, though imperfect, righteousness of life (*iustitia vitae*) as a fruit of this faith. Rom 6:14: "Sin shall not have dominion over you; for ye are not under the Law, but under grace."[164]

Again, being under grace serves as the foundation for everything. The Law that condemns sin will not have dominion over the slave to God. The undeserved favor from God rules over them in Christ. Believers are slaves of righteousness under grace serving the Master and King Jesus through faith in sanctification and serving one another. Slaves of righteousness engage in good and pleasing works.

The slave to God under grace should not go on sinning on account of freedom from slavery to sin. Paul continues and asks another rhetorical question: "What then? Should we sin because we are not under Law, but under grace? May

---

[164] Pieper, *Christian Dogmatics*, vol. 3, 18, 410.

it never come to be!" (Rom 6:15). Freedom from the Law means no longer being an enemy of the Law, but a friend of the Law as a slave of righteousness. Luther comments on Romans 6:14, 15, discussing a human way of Law and the theological way of understanding the Law:

> Here we have Paul's assertion of freedom from the Law. But immediately he raises an objection to himself … This is what he is saying here, namely, that opportunity is made for the flesh if freedom is understood in this fleshly way. We are not free from the Law (as I have said above) in a human way, by which the Law is destroyed and changed, but in a divine and theological way, by which we are changed and from enemies of the Law are made friends of the Law.[165]

Luther seems to describe that the friend of the Law should not desire to sin just because they are free from the Law's demands. Instead, Christians serve and love through faith as a friend of the Law under grace.

Life's Renewal is Newness of Life in Sanctification

God brings sanctification to the righteous through Baptism and faith. Sanctification means "to make holy."[166] Sanctification

---

[165] "Lectures on Galatians Chapters 1-6" (1519), *AE* 27:347; Luther writes "In line with this thought 1 Peter 2:16 also says: ' As free men, yet without using your freedom as a pretext for evil, but as servants [slaves] of God.'" Ibid; Cf. note 154.

[166] Elwell, 1051-54; More precisely, "sanctification is the work of the Holy Spirit of making people holy." Steven P. Mueller, *Called to Believe,*

and purification are given to sinners through faith and Baptism. Romans 6:4 explains that Christians are buried with Christ in Baptism into His death and raised from the dead to walk to live in "life's renewal." Sanctified living is a gift and response to being declared righteous from sin and bound to Christ. The slave to righteousness has been buried and raised with Christ and, as a result, walks in life's renewal, in Christ's life through faith.

Christians are, therefore, exhorted to present their bodily members to God as resurrected from the dead with Christ. Paul exhorts the slave of Christ, "Present yourselves to God as living from [the] dead and your bodily members to God [as] instruments of righteousness" (Rom 6:13). The slave of Christ is "responsiveness to God leading to righteousness" (Rom 6:16) and is to "present your bodily members [as] slavish to righteousness leading to sanctification" (Rom 6:19).

This slavery to God and righteousness looks like a "good" spiritual slavery.[167] The slave to God presents "bodily members" (Rom 6:19) as enslaved to righteousness. Paul writes, "For just as you presented your bodily members [as] slavish to impurity and to a lawless mindset leading to lawless behavior, thus now present your bodily members [as] slavish to righteousness leading to sanctification" (Rom 6:19). In short, slavery to righteousness looks like Christ.

Martin Luther's explanation of alien righteousness, cited above, leads to proper righteousness. He draws from Paul's imperative exhortations to believers to present themselves as slaves to righteousness, leading to sanctification.

> The second kind of righteousness is our proper righteousness, not because we alone

---

Teach, and Confess: An Introduction to Doctrinal Theology, 528.

[167] As a result of being delivered from evil or bad spiritual slavery—slavery to sin and death.

work it, but because we work with that first and alien righteousness … We read in Rom. 6 [:19] that his righteousness is set opposite our own actual sin: "For just as you once yielded your members to impurity and to greater and greater iniquity, so now yield your members to righteousness for sanctification."[168]

Luther's recognition of proper righteousness looks like Paul's imperatives. Yet this "proper righteousness" works from the indicative first—alien righteousness, and is a response to grace.

Fruit for Sanctification

Paul's imperative exhortations urge slaves of righteousness to bring forth fruit for sanctification. There is no fruit for sanctification apart from Christ's righteousness. But with and in Christ, fruit grows from righteousness given. Eternal life is always the outcome for the slave of Christ. Paul writes, "But now after being freed from the [slavery] of sin and after being enslaved to God, you are having your fruit for sanctification, and the outcome is eternal life" (Rom 6:22). Slavery to God and righteousness "looks like" bringing forth "fruit for sanctification" (Rom 6:22), flowing from righteousness given in Christ alone.

---

[168] "Two Kinds of Righteousness" (1519), *AE* 31:300; Luther explains, "Therefore, through the first righteousness arises the voice of the bridegroom who says to the soul, 'I am yours,' but through the second comes the voice of the bride who answers, 'I am yours.' Then the marriage is consummated; it becomes strong and complete in accordance with the Song of Solomon [2:16]: 'My beloved is mine and I am his.' Then the soul no longer seeks to be righteous in and for itself, but it has Christ as its righteousness and therefore seeks only the welfare of others." *AE* 31:300.

Paul exhorts Christians to resist sin (cf. Rom 6:12) and to "present your bodily members [as] slavish to righteousness leading to sanctification" (Rom 6:19). These imperatives derive from the promised outcome of eternal life because the slave to Christ is holy and righteous on account of Christ. Irenaeus remarked about the bodily members in *Against Heresies*: "In these same members, therefore, in which we used to serve sin, and bring forth fruit unto death, does He wish us to [be obedient] unto righteousness, that we may bring forth fruit unto life."[169] Irenaeus accurately describes the responsiveness of Christians and how believers are exhorted to righteousness as slaves of God in Christ, bringing forth fruit in sanctification.

Slaves of Righteousness

The slave to righteousness is responsive from the heart to God's grace in Christ. Paul simply states, "But thanks [be] to God, because you were slaves of sin, but you responded from [the] heart to [the] form of teaching into which you were handed over. And, after being freed from the [slavery] of sin, you were enslaved to righteousness" (Rom 6:17-18). Nygren comments, "The situation of the Christian is described very simply by Paul: He is a slave who has changed masters. Formerly he stood under the dominion of sin; now he is set free from sin, but bound in service to righteousness."[170] Melanchthon wrote of this moral righteousness by imputation:

---

169 Irenaeus, "Against the Heresies," vol. 1, *The Ante-Nicene Fathers*, ed. Alexander Roberts and James Donaldson, 10 vols. (1885–1887; repr., Peabody, MA: Hendrickson, 1994), 542. Hereafter ANF.

170 Anders Nygren, *Commentary on Romans*, (Philadelphia: Fortress Press, 1975), 257.

> For although we are righteous, that is, accepted by imputation on account of Christ, it is necessary that virtue also be begun in us—righteousness, that is obedience. Righteousness brings forth virtues, righteous actions. Nevertheless, we must know that we are righteous on account of Christ, our High Priest, that is, accepted by God not on account of the worthiness of our obedience or qualities.[171]

What Melanchthon calls obedience is a response to Christ's righteousness imputed to the slave of God by grace, and does not originate in any way from the worthiness of the slave.

Franzmann identifies slaves of righteousness as those "liberated from sin and enslaved to righteousness through the word."[172] The Word is Christ in Baptism, and the Word of the proclamation of the Good News in Christ's redemption for sinners. "Consequently, faith [comes] from hearing, and hearing through [the] word of Christ/[the] Messiah" (Rom 10:17). Slaves to sin are liberated from the dominion of sin, death, and Satan in the Good News and are bound to righteousness. The Confessions teach, "Faith is bound to yield good fruits."[173]

Those declared righteous in Christ now serve as slaves to God with thanksgiving and respond with righteous living. For examples of what this entails, one can simply

---

[171] Philip Melanchthon, *Commentary on Romans*, trans. Fred Kramer (St. Louis, MO: Concordia Publishing House, 2010), 151.

[172] Franzmann, *Romans* (St. Louis, MO: Concordia Publishing House, 1968), 115.

[173] Kolb, 41; cf. *AC* VI.1.

look ahead to the lifestyle Paul lays out in Romans 12-16, Ephesians 4-6, Colossians 3-4 and so forth. To be more specific, consider the fruit of the Spirit laid out in Galatians 5:22-23, "The fruit of the Spirit, however, is love, joy, peace, forbearance, kindness, goodness, faithfulness, gentleness, and self-control. The Law is not opposed to such things." Similarly, in the Pastorals, God's virtuous slave to righteousness is explicitly instructed to be kind and patient. Paul writes to Timothy,

> And the Lord's slave must not be quarrelsome, but be kind to all, able to teach, patient when wronged, with gentleness correcting those who are in opposition, if perhaps God may give them repentance leading to the full knowledge of the truth, and they may come to their senses and escape from the snare of the devil, having been held captive by him to do his will. (2 Tim 2:24-26).

Obey Your Master

Paul exhorts believers to obey their master.[174] The one who obeys is responsive to the master. Jesus Christ

---

[174] As to addressing the words obey and obedience: Middendorf writes, "In English "obey" generally conveys the notion of something we must do ... However, the basic biblical sense means to listen and respond appropriately. The underlying Hebrew is usually šəmaʻ lə, "to hearken to," often to the word of Yahweh. The NT uses the Greek word group of ὑπακούω similarly. When one hears God's condemning law, the appropriate response is to acknowledge, that is, confess, that what God says about me and all people apart from Christ is true (e.g., 1 Jn 1:8–10). At times, however, what is mistranslated "obey" is intended to be a receptive response to the gospel ... For example ... Paul even uses the

is the Lord or Master of slaves to righteousness. Slaves to righteousness respond to grace in Christ. As the slave to sin responds to sin, so the slave of God responds to Christ and His righteousness given through faith. Moo writes, "If one is not serving God, then, whether knowingly or not, one is serving sin."[175] That means spiritual slavery can only be *either* to sin, death, and Satan, *or* to God in Christ and his righteousness (cf. Rom 6:15-19).[176] Moo notes, "In

---

verb ὑπακούω as a parallel for πιστεύω in Romans 10:16. Thus, when one hears the gospel, the appropriate response of ὑπακοή is to "listen responsively," to "heed" or "hearken to" it with receptive faith (as in Rom 1:5; 6:16; 15:18; 16:26; cf. Rom 10:9)." Middendorf, "The New Obedience: An Exegetical Glance at Article VI of the Augsburg Confession," *Concordia Journal*, Vol. 41, no. 3 (Summer 2015): 202; cf. 210-19; Cf. *Romans 1-8*, Concordia Commentary, 60, 66–67, 500–501; Paul uses the words such as; ὑπακούειν, υπακουετε, ὑπακοῆς, and ὑπηκούσατε in Romans 6:12, 16, 17, which seem to be from the word, ὑπακούω, which is best described as listening and responding appropriately; However, BDAG renders, "ὑπακοή, ῆς, ἡ … ① a state of being in compliance, *obedience* (one listens and follows instructions) ② gener., the obedience which every slave owes his master εἰς ὑπακοήν= εἰς τὸ ὑπακούειν to obey Ro 6:16a. ⑤ predom. of obedience to God and God's commands, abs. (opp. ἁμαρτία) Ro 6:16b. Cp. 1 Cl 9:3; 19:1. δι' ὑπακοῆς *obediently, in obedience* (toward God) 10:2, 7. Of Christ's obedience Hb 5:8.—W. subjective gen. of Christ's obedience to God Ro 5:19 (opp. παρακοή); of human beings' obedience to the will of God as expressed in the gospel Ro 15:18; 16:19," 1028; "ὑπακούω hupakouō; from G5259 and G191; *to listen, attend to:* — answer." NASEC, G5219.

[175] Douglas Moo, *The New Application Commentary: From Biblical Text … To Contemporary Life* (Grand Rapids, MI: Zondervan, 2000), 212.

[176] "Behold, as the eyes of slaves look to the hand of their master, As the eyes of a servant-girl to the hand of her mistress, So our eyes look to Yahweh our God, Until He is gracious to us" (Psalm 123:2); For the one who trusts in Yahweh on account of Jesus Christ crucified and risen is a slave of God and looks to Yahweh as master. As previously examined in chapter 1, the slavery language in the Old Testament is much like Paul's use of slavery in Romans 6 as the eyes of the believer looks to Yahweh as a slave to a master; See Chapter 1, subheading, Slavery in the Old Testament.

verse 19 the apostle turns to the imperative mode to set out the response that believers should make to the transfer of power ... God has given us a new master, and now we must obey that master."[177]

When Paul writes of slave-master relationships, his hearers would readily understand. Christians are slaves to God in Christ, and some were also slaves to earthly masters. So, whether a slave to an earthly master or not, slaves of Christ are exhorted to respond appropriately to God for the sake of Christ, their Lord and Master.[178] In an interesting note on responding to this change of lordship, Grothe advises, "Paul's words about sanctifying do not lay on Christians a post-Gospel dose of (guilt-producing!) Law. 'Sanctifying' is Gospel talk. The change of lordship transfers sinful man out of that vicious cycle in which he is trapped when trying to be right with God by doing the works of Law."[179] Sinners handed over from the lordship of sin and the Law are sanctified slaves of God in Jesus Christ. Christians live as responsive, joyful, fruit-producing slaves of Christ by grace. Jesus Christ displayed the love of God in dying and rising for sinners, bringing justification for the ungodly. Repented sinners saved by grace live as slaves of

---

[177] Moo, *The New Application Commentary From Biblical Text ... To Contemporary Life*, 210.

[178] Paul writes: "Slaves, be obedient to those who are your 1masters according to the flesh, with fear and trembling, in the integrity of your heart, as to Christ; not by way of eyeservice, as men-pleasers, but as slaves of Christ, doing the will of God from the heart, serving with good will as to the Lord, and not to men, knowing that whatever good thing each one does, this he will receive back from the Lord, whether slave or free. And masters, do the same things to them, giving up threatening, knowing that both their Master and yours is in heaven, and there is no partiality with Him" (Eph 6:5-9; cf. Col 3:2; 1 Tim 6:1; Tit 2:9).

[179] Grothe, *The Justification of the Ungodly: An Interpretation of Romans*, 2nd ed., 298.

righteousness in obedience to their new Lord and Master, Jesus Christ. Thus, Paul's imperatives to slaves of God in Romans 6 are the Master Jesus' will for His redeemed slaves so they respond appropriately in ways that bless their own lives, as well as that of their neighbors, all to the glory of God.

Conclusion

Slavery to God and righteousness in Christ looks like walking in life's renewal as responsive slaves of Christ to imperatives, based upon the indicative declaration of righteousness through faith and Baptism into Christ. The struggle to resist the reign of sin in the mortal body remains now and will be so until the Last Day. Then when sin and impurity will be no more, as the "former things have passed away" (Rev 21:4; cf. Rev 21).

Nevertheless, Paul writes, "Therefore if anyone is in Christ, he is a new creation; the old things passed away; behold, new things have come" (2 Cor 5:17). The new creature of God is already now and entails being a slave under Christ's righteousness. Jesus Christ is the Lord and Master of the slaves of righteousness, and the slave to Christ responds appropriately to the Masters' exhortations. As Paul explains in Romans 6, this means presenting one's body as an instrument of righteousness, producing fruit for sanctification that leads to eternal life, eternal life in Christ alone. The slave to God is dead to the reign of sin through Baptism into Christ, "For the payment of sin is death, but the gracious gift of God is eternal life in Christ Jesus our Lord" (Rom 6:23).

As members of the Body of Christ, slaves to God are extensions of the Master Jesus Christ. Lenski comments, "The fact that we are still slaving as slaves we have seen in 6:16–22, [identifies] also that this is a voluntary slavery of emancipated slaves in expectation, not of death, but of life everlasting, thus a joyous, blessed slavery."[180] The slave to Christ lives in Christ's joy and then becomes a "slave to all." Slaves of God are raised in life's renewal in Christ, living in the fruits of sanctification, now and forever, all on account of Christ Jesus, the only begotten Son of God, Redeemer, and Savior of all mankind.

---

[180] Lenski, *The Interpretation of St. Paul's Epistle to the Romans*, 455–457.

St. Paul (Second State) (1514), by Albrecht Dürer

Flagellation of Christ (1512), from "The Passion," Engraving by Albrecht Dürer

Conclusion

It is a stark "reality" that all are spiritual slaves—"if" is not an option, only whom you serve. All of mankind has been bound to sin and death ever since the Fall. Slavery to sin plagues the entire world. Those who reject the Word of God remain slaves to sin. Yes, all men are slaves to sin and death, but, by the grace of God, there is another option. Since Jesus fully paid the redemption price for all, a blessed slavery becomes possible, one which really means belonging to God and His righteousness—nothing more or less. Those who receive grace, listen and respond to the Word of the crucified and risen Lord Jesus Christ and become slaves to God and His righteousness. Romans 6 contrasts the sinner in bondage to sin under the Law and the sinner/saint in bondage to Christ and righteousness under grace. In regard to the latter, Paul uses slavery language in both indicative and imperative statements for Christians to comprehend through faith.

Chapter One asserted that Paul's slavery language should be understood in the context of slavery in the Greco-Roman era. That slavery reveals temporal worldly slavery and oppression from men. Slavery in the Old Testament was also evident among God's people, especially when other nations enslaved Israel, such as the Egyptians and

Babylonians. However, slavery in the Bible should not be simplistically equated to the American experience. Yet looking at slavery in the past and present helps us understand the reality of spiritual slavery.

Both the Old and New Testaments then speak of a spiritual aspect of slavery to sin and slavery to God. This thesis explores how worldly slavery both compares and stands in contrast with spiritual slavery to sin, as well as becoming enslaved to God and righteousness. Looking at slavery in the past, present, and future helps us understand the reality of spiritual slavery. However, slavery to God certainly is not equivalent to slavery around the world, then or now.

Chapter Two depicted how spiritual slavery to sin aptly describes the condition of sinners. The slave to sin can only produce bad fruit (cf. Rom 6:21). And those enslaved to sin owe the payment of death (cf. Rom 6:23). As the slave to sin commits sin and evil deeds, the slave to sin is respondent and obedient to sin under Law (Rom 6:14). When under Law, the slave to sin is an instrument for unrighteousness (cf. Rom 6:13). All sinners are condemned under Law, and the payment of sin is death for the sinner forever.

Chapter Three describes how those who were Baptized into Christ are justified and declared righteous. God's declaration of righteousness for the ungodly sinner comes through Christ's death and resurrection and is given in Baptism. Those Baptized into Christ Jesus are now under grace, freed from the reign of sin and living with Christ (cf. Rom 6:3-8). Paul says they are still slaves, but now of God and righteousness who live in sanctification now and forever. Thus, we have seen that slavery language describes both the condemned slave to sin, and the slave of God in

Christ who has been redeemed from the condemnation of sin in Baptism.

The sinner is freed from slavery to sin on account of Christ and declared righteous from sin. The sinner is dead, entombed, and raised with Christ in Baptism—having died and risen with Christ, stands justified and declared righteous from sin. The slave to sin has been freed from enslavement to sin and death, and becomes a slave to God. This involves a transfer of power, or being handed over (cf. Rom 6:17-18) to a new master, the Lord Jesus Christ. Redeemed slaves of God and righteousness are united and grow together in Christ's death and resurrection under grace.

Chapter Four presented what slavery to God and righteousness in Christ "looks like." "Baptism ends the slavery (now), but begins the battle (not yet)."[181] Therefore, imperative exhortations are given to those who live already now in Christ's righteousness (cf. Rom 6:12-23). They are empowered by the indicative declarations of grace in Christ. The slave of God struggles with sin in the temporal body and is given the imperative to resist the reign of sin (cf. Rom 6:12). This struggle shows how the slave to Christ is *simul iustus et peccator.* The slave to Christ and righteousness responds positively to the indicative of grace as instruments of righteousness who are called to walk in life's renewal (cf. Rom 6:4, 12-15). A Christian is a slave through vocational callings in life, which serve and honor God by serving others. The slave to God in Christ produces fruit for sanctification (*holiness,* cf. 6:22) from the Holy Spirit, which leads to eternal life.

In summary, Baptism and faith received in Christ forever seal, bind, and enslave the sinner to God and his

---

[181] Middendorf and Mark Schuler, *Called by the Gospel: An Introduction to the New Testament* (Eugene, OR: Wipf & Stock, 2009), 188.

righteousness. The slave to God has been forgiven of all sin, declared righteous and free from enslavement to sin on account of Christ. Those joyfully bound to God in Christ are responsive instruments of righteousness for now and forever.

Man of Sorrows with Hands Raised/Arms Outstretched (1500), by Albrecht Dürer

Head of Christ Crowned with Thorns (1510),
by Lucas Cranach the Elder

BIBLIOGRAPHY

Arndt, William, Frederick W. Danker, Walter Bauer, et al., *A Greek-English Lexicon of the New Testament and Other Early Christian Literature.* 3rd ed. Chicago: University of Chicago Press, 2000.

——————. *A Greek-English Lexicon of the New Testament and Other Early Christian Literature.* 2nd ed. Chicago: University of Chicago Press, 1979.

Austen, Ralph A. "The Trans-Saharan Slave Trade: A Tentative Census." *Uncommon Market; Essays in the Economic History of the Atlantic Slave Trade.* Ed. by H.A. Gemery and J.A. Hogendorn, 23-76 (1979).

Baucham, Voddie T. *It's Not Like Being Black.* New York, Regnery Faith, 2024.

——————. *Fault Lines.* Salem Books, Washington, D.C., 2021.

Bonhoeffer, Dietrich. *The Cost of Discipleship.* New York: Touchstone, 1995.

Brown, Francis, William Gesenius, S. R. Driver, and Charles A. Briggs. *A Hebrew and English lexicon of the Old Testament, with an appendix containing the biblical Aramaic.* Oxford: Clarendon, 1951.

Cockburn, Andrew. "21st-Century Slaves" *National Geographic*, 204, no. 3 (September 2003): 2–25.

Dare, Rev. Paul. *Christians In A Woke World: A Call to Courage, Confession, and Love.* Independently Published, 2021.

Das, Andrew. *Galatians.* Edited by Dean O. Wenthe, Concordia Commentary. Saint Louis, MO: Concordia Publishing House, 2014.

Dunn, James D. G. *Romans.* Nashville: Thomas Nelson, 2003.

––––––. *Word Biblical Commentary. Romans 1-8.* Vol. 38A. Grand Rapids, MI: Zondervan, 1988.

Elwell, Walter A. *Evangelical Dictionary of Theology.* 2nd ed. Grand Rapids, MI: Baker Academic, 2001.

English Standard Version (ESV). Wheaton, IL: Crossway Bibles, 2016.

Franzmann, Martin H. *Romans.* Concordia Commentary. St. Louis, MO: Concordia Publishing House, 1968.

Gerhard, Johann. *On the End of the World and Hell.* Theological Commonplaces. St. Louis, Mo: Concordia Publishing House, 2021.

Global Slavery Index. "Resource Downloads." Accessed 05/06/2022 and 01/26/2023. https://www.globalslaveryindex.org/resources/downloads/.

Grothe, Jonathan F. *The Justification of the Ungodly: An Interpretation of Romans.* 2nd ed. St. Catharines, Ontario, Canada, 2012.

Harris, Jon. *Christianity and Social Justice: Religions in Conflict.* Ann Arbor, Michigan: Reformation Zion Publishing, 2021.

Heiser, Michael S., and Vincent M. Setterholm. *Glossary of Morpho-Syntactic Database Terminology.* Lexham Press, 2013.

Hezser, Catherine. *Jewish Slavery in Antiquity.* Oxford: Oxford University Press, 2009.

Henkel, Socrates, and Ambrose. Revised by W. F. Lehmann. Schmidt, Jon Alan, ed./trans. *The Book of Concord of 1580*, 1854, Accessed 04/20/2022. https://www.1580boc.org/ap/xx-viii.

Holladay, William L., W. Baumgartner, and Ludwig Koehler. *A Concise Hebrew and Aramaic Lexicon of the Old Testament*. Grand Rapids: William B. Eerdmans Pub, 1971.

Holmes, Michael W. *The Apostolic Fathers: Greek Texts and English Translations*. 3rd ed. Grand Rapids, MI: Baker Academic, 2007.

Horton, Michael S. *Justification*. New Studies in Dogmatics. Grand Rapids, Michigan: Zondervan, 2018.

Joshel, Sandra. *Slavery in the Roman World*. Cambridge: Cambridge University Press, 2010.

Kittel, Gerhard and Geoffrey W. Bromiley. *Theological Dictionary of the New Testament*. Vol 2. Grand Rapids, MI: W.B. Eerdmans, 1964.

------. Gerhard Friedrich and Geoffrey W. Bromiley. *Theological Dictionary of the New Testament: Abridged in One Volume*. Grand Rapids, MI: W.B. Eerdmans, 1985.

Kolb, Robert and Timothy J. Wengert, eds. *The Book of Concord: The Confessions of the Evangelical Lutheran Church*. Minneapolis, MN: Fortress Press, 2000.

Kretzmann, Paul E. *Popular Commentary of the Bible: The New Testament*. 2 vols. St. Louis: Concordia, [1921]–[1922?].

Legacy Standard Bible (LSB). La Habra, CA: The Lockman Foundation/Three Sixteen Publishing, 2021.

Lenski, Richard C. H. *Interpretation of St Paul's Epistle to the Romans*. Minneapolis, MN: Augsburg Fortress, 2008.

Liddell, Henry and Robert Scott. *A Greek-English Lexicon*. 9th ed. Oxford: Oxford University Press, 1996

Lueker, Erwin. *Lutheran Cyclopedia*. St. Louis, MO: Concordia Publishing House, 1975.

Luther, Martin. *Luther's Works, American Edition*. Vols 1–30, edited by Jaroslav Pelikan. St. Louis, MO: Concordia Publishing House, 1955–76. Vols. 31–55 edited by Helmut Lehmann. Philadelphia/Minneapolis: Muhlenberg/Fortress, 1957–86. Vols. 56–82, edited by Christopher Boyd Brown and Benjamin T. G. Mayes. St. Louis, MO: Concordia, 2009–.

Lutheran Service Book. St. Louis, MO: Concordia Publishing House, 2006.

Mangum, Douglas. *The Lexham Glossary of Theology*. Bellingham, WA: Lexham Press, 2014.

Martin, Dale. *Slavery As Salvation: The Metaphor of Slavery in Pauline Christianity*. Eugene, OR: Wipf and Stock, 1990.

Melanchthon, Philip. *Commentary on Romans*. Translated by Fred Kramer. St. Louis, MO: Concordia Publishing House, 2010.

Middendorf, Michael P. *Romans 1-8*. St. Louis, MO: Concordia Publishing House, 2013.

———. *Romans 9-16*. St. Louis, MO: Concordia Publishing House, 2016.

———. "The New Obedience: An Exegetical Glance at Article VI of the Augsburg Confession." *Concordia Journal*. Vol. 41, no. 3 (Summer 2015): 201-19.

———. *The "I" in the Storm: A Study of Romans 7*. St. Louis, MO: Concordia Academic Press, 1997.

—————— and Mark Schuler. *Called by the Gospel: An Introduction to the New Testament*. Eugene, OR: Wipf & Stock, 2009.

McKim, Donald K. *The Westminster Dictionary of Theological Terms*, 2nd ed. Revised and Expanded. Louisville, KY: Westminster John Knox Press, 2014.

Moo, Douglas J, *Encountering the Book of Romans: A Theological Survey*. 2nd ed. Grand Rapids, MI: Baker Academic, 2014.

――――. *Romans. The New Application Commentary: From Biblical Text … To Contemporary Life*. Grand Rapids, MI: Zondervan, 2000.

――――. *The Letter to the Romans*. 2nd ed. *The New International Commentary of the New Testament*. Grand Rapids, MI: Wm. B. Eerdmans Publishing Co., 2018.

The New International Version (NIV). Grand Rapids, MI: Zondervan, 2011.

Noll, Mark. *The Civil War as a Theological Crisis*. North Carolina: The University of North Carolina Press, 2006.

Nordling, John G. *Philemon*. St. Louis, MO: Concordia Publishing House, 2004.

――――. "Slaves to God, Slaves to One Another." *Concordia Theological Quarterly* 80, no. 3-4 (July/October 2016): 231-50.

Nygren, Anders. *Commentary on Romans*. Philadelphia: Fortress Press, 1975.

Pieper, Francis. *Christian Dogmatics*. Vol. 1-3. St. Louis, MO: Concordia Publishing House, 1953.

Pond, Clifford. *Born Slaves: An easier-to-read and abridged version of the classic "The Bondage of the Will" by Martin Luther, first published in 1525*. Edited by J. P. Arthur and H. J. Appleby. London, England: Grace Publication Trust, 1998.

Scaer, David P. *Baptism*. Confessional Lutheran Dogmatics, Vol. 11. St. Louis, MO: The Luther Academy, 1999.

————. *A Latin Ecclesiastical Glossary: For Francis Pieper's Christian Dogmatics*, 1978.

Schreiner, Thomas R. *Romans*. 2nd ed. *Baker Exegetical Commentary on the New Testament*. Grand Rapids, MI: Baker Academic, 2018.

Scheidel, Walter. "Quantifying the Sources of Slaves in the Early Roman Empire" *Journal of Roman Studies* 87 (1997): 156-159.

Strong, James. *A Concise Dictionary of the Words in the Greek Testament and The Hebrew Bible*. Bellingham, WA: Logos Bible Software, 2009.

The Ante-Nicene Fathers. Edited by Alexander Roberts and James Donaldson. 10 vols. 1885-1887. Reprint, Peabody, MA: Hendrickson, 2004.

The Nicene and Post-Nicene Fathers. First Series. Edited by Philip Schaff. 14 vols. 1886-1889. Grand Rapids, MI: Hendrickson, 1997.

The Nicene and Post-Nicene Fathers. Second Series. Edited by Philip Schaff and Henry Wace. 14 vols. 1890-1900. Reprint, Peabody, MA: Hendrickson, 1961.

Think Africa. "The Slave Trade in Black Africans" Accessed 05/11/2022. https://thinkafrica.net/atlantic-slave-trade/.

Walther, C. F. W. *The Proper Distinction between Law and Gospel: Thirty-Nine Evening Lectures*. Translated by W. H. T. Dau. St. Louis: Concordia, 1929.

Wilkon, Todd, "Is the Law Bad." *Issues Etc.* (2016): 5-17. Accessed 05/09/2022. https://podcast.issuesetc.org/winter2016.pdf.

Zondervan Bible Publishers, edited by Robert L. Thomas. *The Strongest NASB Exhaustive Concordance*. Grand Rapids, Michigan: Zondervan, 2004.

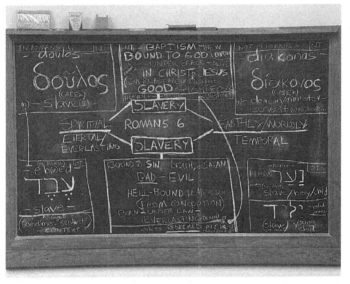

Chalkboard notes, and pic from Bible Study on
Bound To God in Christ Jesus taught on this book
at fieldwork congregation Summer/Fall 2024

ABOUT THE AUTHOR

Nathan Tritch earned a BS in Biblical Theology and Religion in 2018 at Liberty University, MA in Theology at Concordia Irvine in 2022, and currently enrolled as an MDiv student at Concordia Seminary in St. Louis. MO.